RAMADAN GEMS

30 Ways to Maximize Ramadan

Published by:

23-2 Jalan PJS 5/30, Petaling Jaya Commercial City
46150 Petaling Jaya, Selangor, Malaysia
+603-7772-3156 (office) / +6017-399-7411 (mobile)
info@tertib.press
www.tertib.press
@tertibpress (Facebook & Instagram)

Author	:	Yahya Ibrahim
Transcriber	:	Aliya Raihanah Azhar Hanis Hanani Mohammad Tahir
Editor	:	Najibah Nasruddin
Cover design	:	Faris Akmal bin Faizal
Book design	:	Abdul Adzim Md Daim
Printed by	:	Firdaus Press Sdn. Bhd.

RAMADAN GEMS

First Edition: April 2021

Perpustakaan Negara Malaysia Cataloguing-in-Publication Data

Yahya Adel Ibrahim
Ramadan Gems / Yahya Adel Ibrahim.
ISBN 978-967-2420-99-6
1. Ramadan.
2. Prayer--Islam.
3. Islam--Customs and practices.
I. Title.
297.362

Contents

Foreword

A day in Ramadan is observed as a day of opportunities and chances to gain the most out of the blessed month. It is a beautiful month where Allah grants multifold rewards and special moments for certain actions to be carried out specially in Ramadan. Take these short reminders day by day as part of the preparation and practices for Ramadan, with the intention to obtain the most benefits and *barakah* out of it.

Tertib Publishing

Preface

السَّلَامُ عَلَيْكُمْ وَرَحْمَةُ اللهِ وَبَرَكَاتُهُ

Assalamualaikum wa rahmatullahi wa barakatuh.

All praises to Allah for another chance of encountering Ramadan, and embracing this holy month of blessings. *Ramadan Gems* is a miniature collection of *dhikr, du'a,* tips, and reminders that can be practiced throughout Ramadan, and may also be performed during specific times of the month. This book has been arranged in a way that allows its readers to read a chapter every day throughout the month of Ramadan, or the whole book in one sitting as an effort to prepare for the entire month.

May these reminders be beneficial for us and, through its practice, grant us the highest levels of *Jannah*, along with Prophet Muhammad ﷺ and those who are dear to him. May Allah accept our fasts in this blessed month of Ramadan. *Allahumma ameen*.

DAY 1

The Great *Dhikr*

One of the greatest *dhikr* of Allah سبحانه و تعالى is to say:

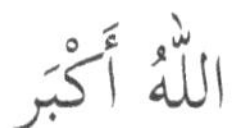

Allahu Akbar

Allah is The Greatest

Occasionally, within the modern context of our time, this statement has been misused by different outlets and people who do not know enough about Islam and Muslims. It is sometimes portrayed in movies and other popular mediums as a war cry, or a chant of destruction.

Conversely, saying, "*Allahu Akbar,*" (اللهُ أَكْبَر) affirms that there is nothing greater than Allah. There is no majesty greater than Allah. There is no difficulty in life that Allah would not able to fix. There is no success that we acquire that is greater than Allah. There is no success that is greater than to have it been granted by Allah سبحانه و تعالى Himself. Let this *dhikr* be something that resonates within our hearts; in times of happiness and sorrow. Let us always recite, "*Allahu Akbar,*" (اللهُ أَكْبَر) as an effort to affirm that Allah سبحانه و تعالى is the greatest reality in our life.

May Allah سبحانه و تعالى guide us in the month of Ramadan. May Allah guide us to choose Him and make Him the greatest aspect in our life, by choosing what He has made *halal*, and staying away from what He has made *haram*.

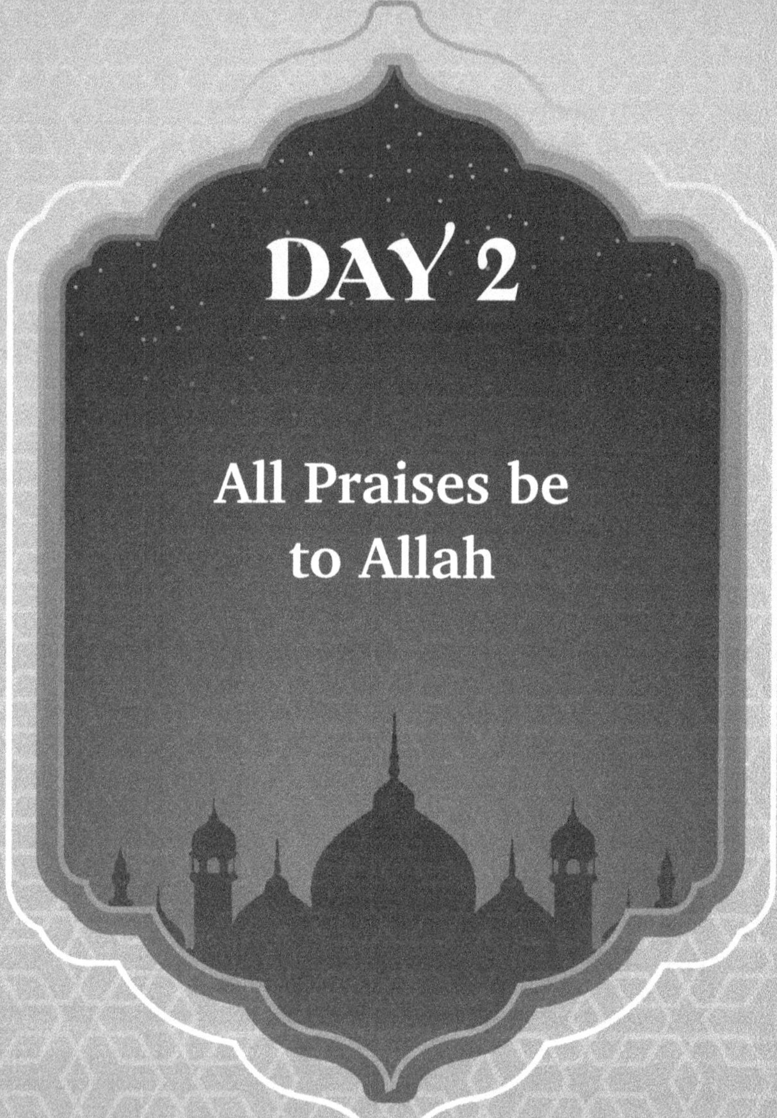

DAY 2

All Praises be to Allah

One of the greatest *dhikr* of Allah سبحانه و تعالى that we can recite on this blessed day of Ramadan is to say:

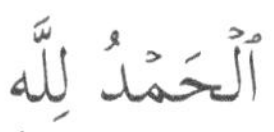

Alhamdulillah

All praises are due to Allah

This is one of the earliest statements that we find in the Qur'an. From the beginning, on the very first page, we hear Allah سبحانه و تعالى command us in His most beautiful *surah*. The *surah* that is most comprehensive.

بِسْمِ ٱللَّهِ ٱلرَّحْمَٰنِ ٱلرَّحِيمِ ﴿١﴾ ٱلْحَمْدُ لِلَّهِ رَبِّ ٱلْعَٰلَمِينَ ﴿٢﴾

Bismillahir Rahmanir Rahim (1) Alhamdulillahi Rabbil 'Alamin (2)

In the Name of Allah, the Most Compassionate, Most Merciful. (1) All praise is for Allah, the Lord of all worlds (2)(*Surah Al Fatihah*, 1: 1-2)

The *dhikr* '*alhamdulillah*' was one of the first statements that Adam عليه السلام stated when his soul entered his body. When Allah commanded for his soul, Adam عليه السلام sneezed and said, "*Alhamdulillah*," and the angels responded, "*Yarhamkallah*. May Allah have mercy upon you."

It is natural *fitrah* for a believer to be thankful to Allah سبحانه و تعالى and praising Him. Therefore, let us make the effort to conclude all of the actions we carry out in life with that statement. Whenever we eat or drink; whenever we are happy or experience sorrow; always say '*alhamdulillah*.' May Allah make us among those who always praise Him throughout the day.

DAY 3

Blessings upon Prophet Muhammad ﷺ

Sallallahu 'alaihi wa sallam

May the peace and blessings of Allah be sent upon him (Prophet Muhammad) (*Sunan an-Nasa'i* 1292)

We ought to remind ourselves to recite the *dhikr* of Allah سبحانه و تعالى that sends peace and blessings to our *Nabi* Muhammad *sallallahu 'alaihi wa sallam* (صَلَّى اللهُ عَلَيْهِ وَسَلَّم). May the blessings of Allah سبحانه و تعالى be sent upon him. May the peace of Allah سبحانه و تعالى descend upon him. In one of his *hadith*, Prophet Muhammad ﷺ said, "The stingiest of people are those who hear that I have been mentioned; however, does not send benedictions upon me." (*Jami' at-Tirmidhi* 3546). *Sallallahu 'alaihi wa sallam* (صَلَّى اللهُ عَلَيْهِ وَسَلَّم). In another *hadith*, we learn that there is no *du'a* that is more elevated than the one that contains salutations upon Prophet Muhammad ﷺ, and there is no *du'a* that is unheard, except the one that does not mention him, *sallallahu 'alaihi wa sallam*. (صَلَّى اللهُ عَلَيْهِ وَسَلَّم) (*Sunan an-Nasa'i* 1292).

Therefore, let us elevate our *ibadah* with the mentioning of Prophet Muhammad ﷺ. Notice that no prayer we make; neither *Fajr*, *Dhuhr*, *'Asr*, *Maghrib* nor

Isha' will be accepted unless we say:

اللهُمَّ صَلِّ عَلَى مُحَمَّدٍ وَعَلَى آلِ مُحَمَّدٍ، كَما صَلَّيْتَ عَلَى إبرَاهِيمَ وَعَلَى آلِ إبرَاهِيمَ، وَبَارِكْ عَلَى مُحَمَّدٍ وَعَلَى آلِ مُحَمَّدٍ، كَما بَارَكْتَ عَلَى إِبْرَاهِيمَ وَعَلَى آلِ إِبْرَاهِيمَ فِي العَالَمِينَ إِنَّكَ حَمِيدٌ مَجِيدٌ

Allahumma salli 'ala Muhammad, wa 'ala āli Muhammad, kama sallaita 'ala Ibrahim, wa 'ala āli Ibrahim, wa bārik 'ala Muhammad wa 'ala āli Muhammad kama barakta 'ala Ibrahim wa 'ala āli Ibrahim, fil 'alamina innaka hamidun majid. (*Sahih Bukhari* 3370)

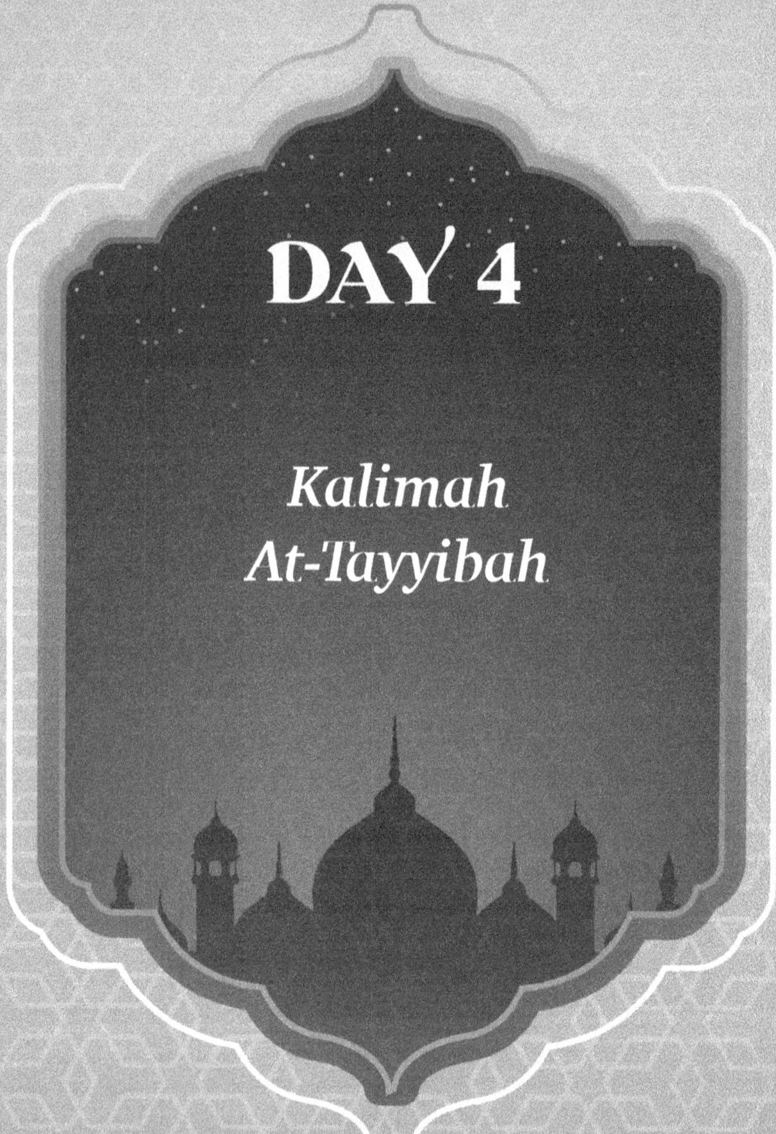

DAY 4

Kalimah At-Tayyibah

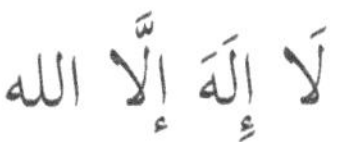

La ilāha illAllah

There is nothing worthy of worship but Allah s.w.t (*Sunan Tirmidhi* 3383)

Another *dhikr* that is taught to us is the *kalimah 'la ilāha illAllah'* (لَا إِلَـٰهَ إِلَّا الله). It is *'kalimah at-tayyibah'*. It is the most beautiful phrase a person can recite; to say that there is none that is worthy of worship except Allah. There is nothing worthy of worship but Allah سبحانه و تعالى .

In a *hadith*, Prophet Muhammad ﷺ said that this is the best *dhikr* for the remembrance of Allah. (*Jami' at-Tirmidhi* 3383) It is *'miftah al-jannah'*, the key that leads to paradise. Thus, we should say it in abundance. The phrase *'la ilāha illAllah'* (لَا إِلَـٰهَ إِلَّا الله) is also part of our formal prayers, and the *adhan*; the call for prayer. It is part of everything that leads us to Allah سبحانه و تعالى . In addition, *la ilāha illAllah* (لَا إِلَـٰهَ إِلَّا الله) is often attached to the phrase *'Muhammad ur-Rasulullah'*, which means Prophet Muhammad is the Messenger of Allah ﷺ.

May Allah سبحانه و تعالى make us among those who honour Him by obeying the teachings of our *Nabi* Muhammad ﷺ. May Allah accept our fasts on this blessed day of Ramadan.

DAY 5

Overcoming Difficulties

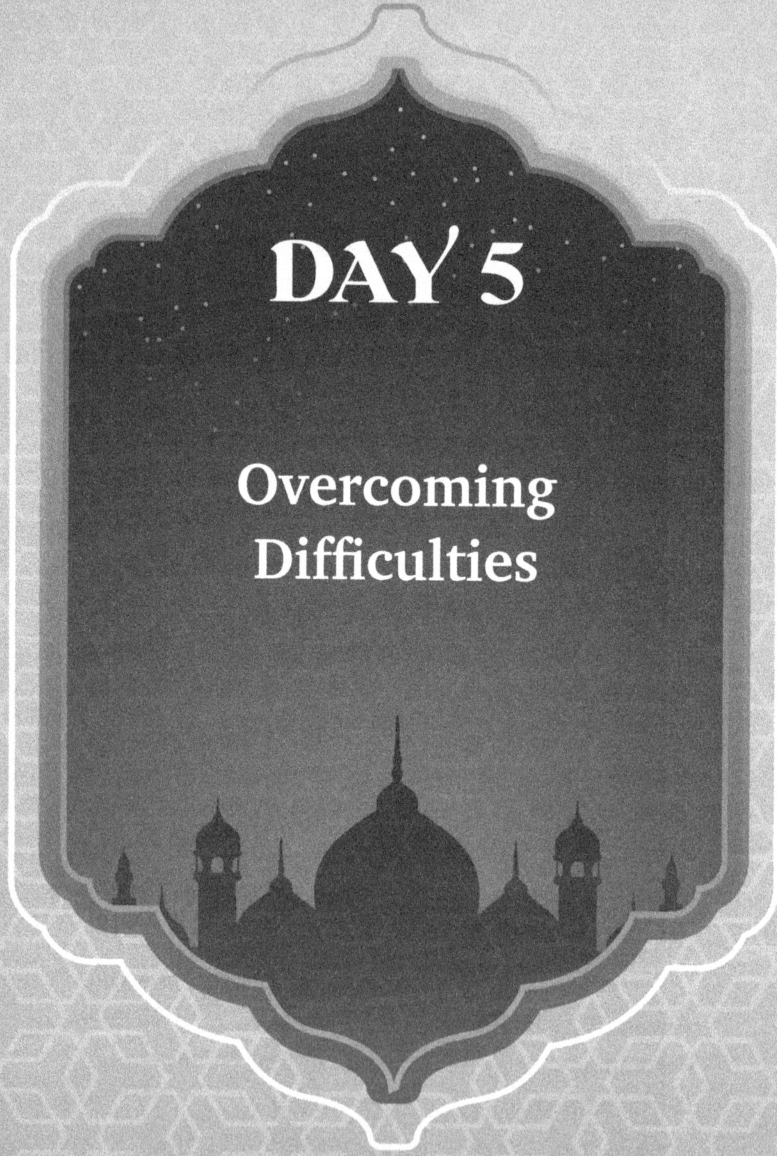

Innalillahi wa inna ilaihi raji'un

Surely to Allah we belong and to Him we will all return. (*Surah Al Baqarah*, 2:156)

Another form of reminder for us in this blessed month of Ramadan, which can bring light and *barakah* into our homes, is the *dhikr*, "*Innalillahi wa inna ilaihi raji'un.*"

When anything difficult happens in our life, remember that we belong to Allah, and to Him we shall return. This statement is taken from the Qur'an and *sunnah* of Prophet Muhammad ﷺ in *surah Al-Baqarah*. Allah promises that He will test us in our life. After listing the different tests that shall occur in our health, wealth, prosperity, and happiness; Allah says:

وَبَشِّرِ ٱلصَّٰبِرِينَ ﴿١٥٥﴾ ٱلَّذِينَ إِذَآ
أَصَٰبَتۡهُم مُّصِيبَةٞ قَالُوٓاْ إِنَّا لِلَّهِ وَإِنَّآ إِلَيۡهِ
رَٰجِعُونَ ﴿١٥٦﴾ أُوْلَٰٓئِكَ عَلَيۡهِمۡ

صَلَوَاتٌ مِّن رَّبِّهِمْ وَرَحْمَةٌ وَأُولَٰٓئِكَ هُمُ
ٱلْمُهْتَدُونَ ﴿١٥٧﴾

> Give good news to those who patiently endure (155) who, when faced with a disaster, say, "Surely to Allah we belong and to Him we will all return." (156) They are the ones who will receive Allah's blessings and mercy. And it is they who are rightly guided. (157) (*Surah Al Baqarah*, 2: 155-157)

Give good news to those who are patient; they are those who, when Allah tests them with calamity, they say, "To Allah we belong, and to Him we shall return." It is upon them that the benedictions and blessings of their Lord will descend.

May Allah make us among them, and keep us firm and steadfast in our faith as we endure the difficulties we face in life. May Allah make us among those who are ever mindful of the knowledge that we come from Allah, and to Him we shall return.

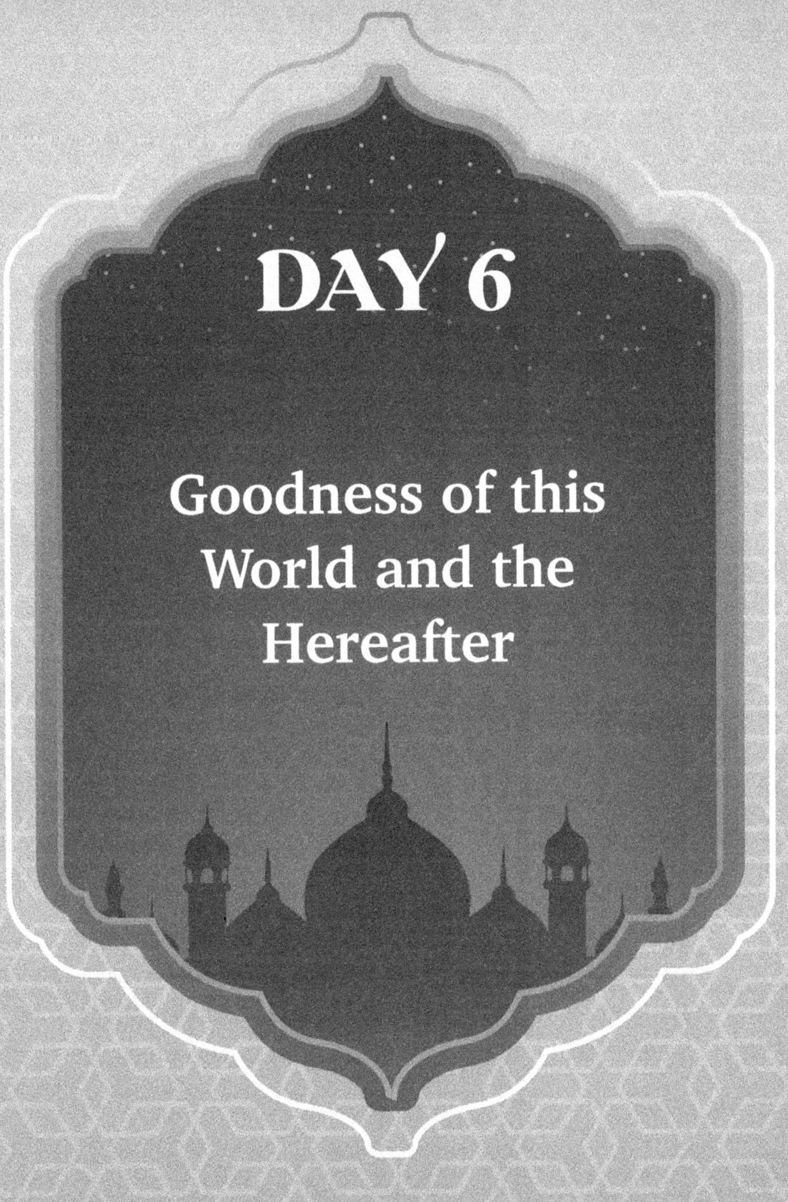
DAY 6
Goodness of this World and the Hereafter

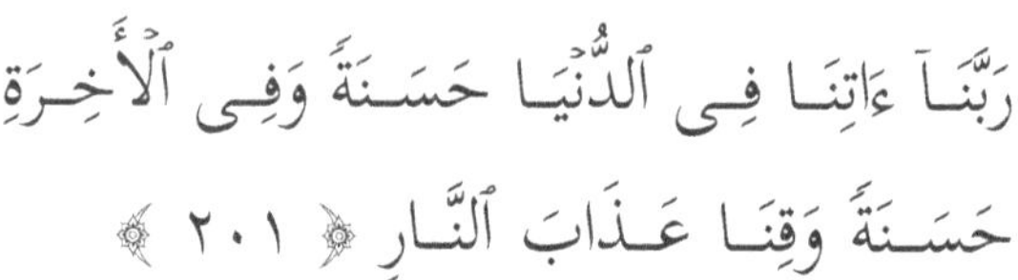

Rabbana ātina fiddunya hasanah wa fil ākhirati hasanah wa qina adhabannar

Our Lord! Grant us the good of this world and the Hereafter, and protect us from the torment of the Fire. (*Surah Al Baqarah*, 2:201)

Prophet Muhammad ﷺ has always reminded us the importance of making *du'a*. There are various *du'a* that are more appropriate or beneficial to be made at specific times of the day or moments, such as those included in this book. This *du'a* was made most by Prophet Muhammad ﷺ during his *tawaf*. It demonstrates how beautiful and meaningful this *du'a* is. It is a statement from the Qur'an where Allah سبحانه و تعالى says that those whose hearts are connected with Him, they would recite the *du'a* above.

"O Allah, grant us goodness in this worldly life, and grant us goodness in the next life. O Allah, protect us from the punishment of the Hellfire." This *du'a* may be broken down into several details. First, we should always ask for goodness in this life. No one would wish to have a difficult life. Therefore, we should ask for goodness in our family, our jobs, our homes, our *iman*, and in our prayers.

Second, we should always ask for Allah سبحانه و تعالى to double the goodness and reward in the Hereafter. Therefore, the next part of the verse is, "...and save us from the punishment of *Jahannam*, and grant us goodness in the next life." O Allah, give us goodness in the next life, and save us from the punishment of the Hellfire. We want *Jannah*, but we also need to ask for protection from the Hellfire. May Allah سبحانه و تعالى bless our days and nights with Qur'an recitation and the act of making lots of *du'a*.

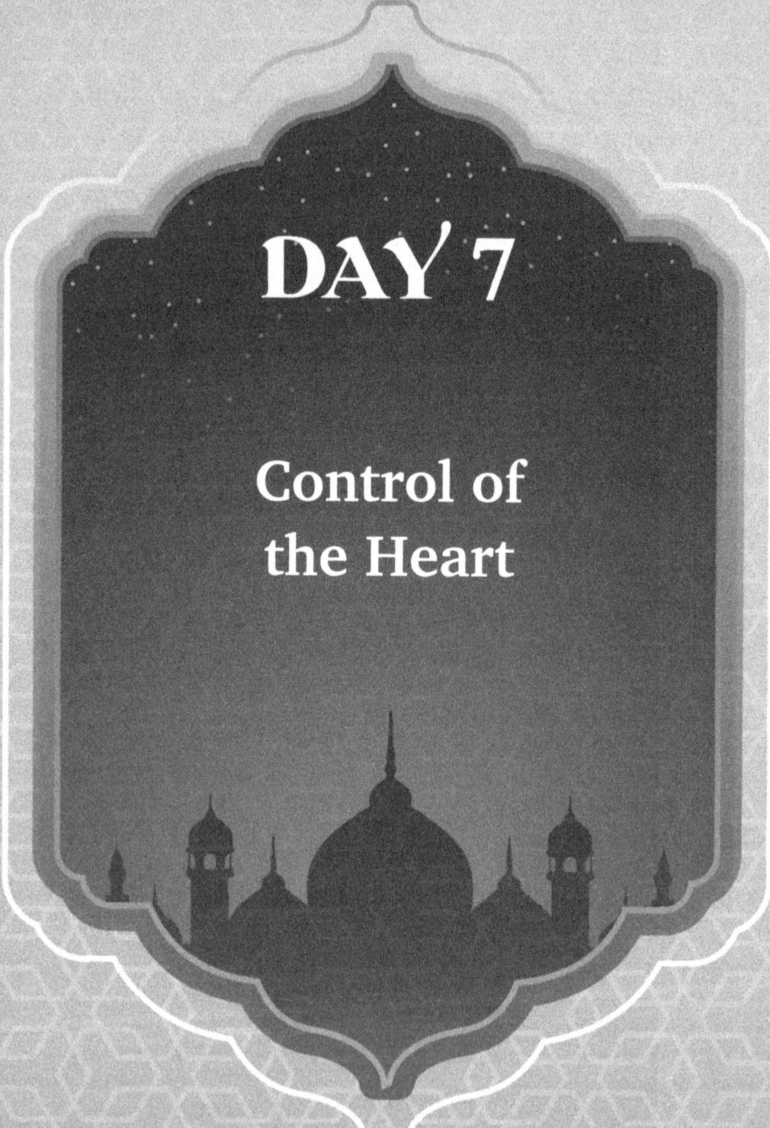

DAY 7

Control of the Heart

Ya muqallibal qulub thabbit qalbi ‘ala diinik

O Changer of the Hearts! Strengthen my heart upon Your Religion. (*Jami‘ at-Tirmidhi* 2140)

This is a great *du‘a* to make on this blessed day of Ramadan, as well as other days. It is a *du‘a* of the Prophet Muhammad ﷺ.

Ummu Salamah رضـي الله عنـه, the wife of Prophet Muhammad ﷺ, would say, “One of the most made *du‘a* Prophet Muhammad ﷺ recited in private was, ‘O Allah, the One who keeps the heart firm, I ask You to keep my heart steadfast upon Your faith.” (*Jami‘ at-Tirmidhi* 3522) This *du‘a* reminds us the importance of remaining faithful to Allah, and how easily our faith can deviate. It is clear that even Prophet Muhammad ﷺ feared this, and would make the *du‘a* as an effort to protect himself, “O Allah, keep my heart firm upon the truth, and keep it steadfast upon it.”

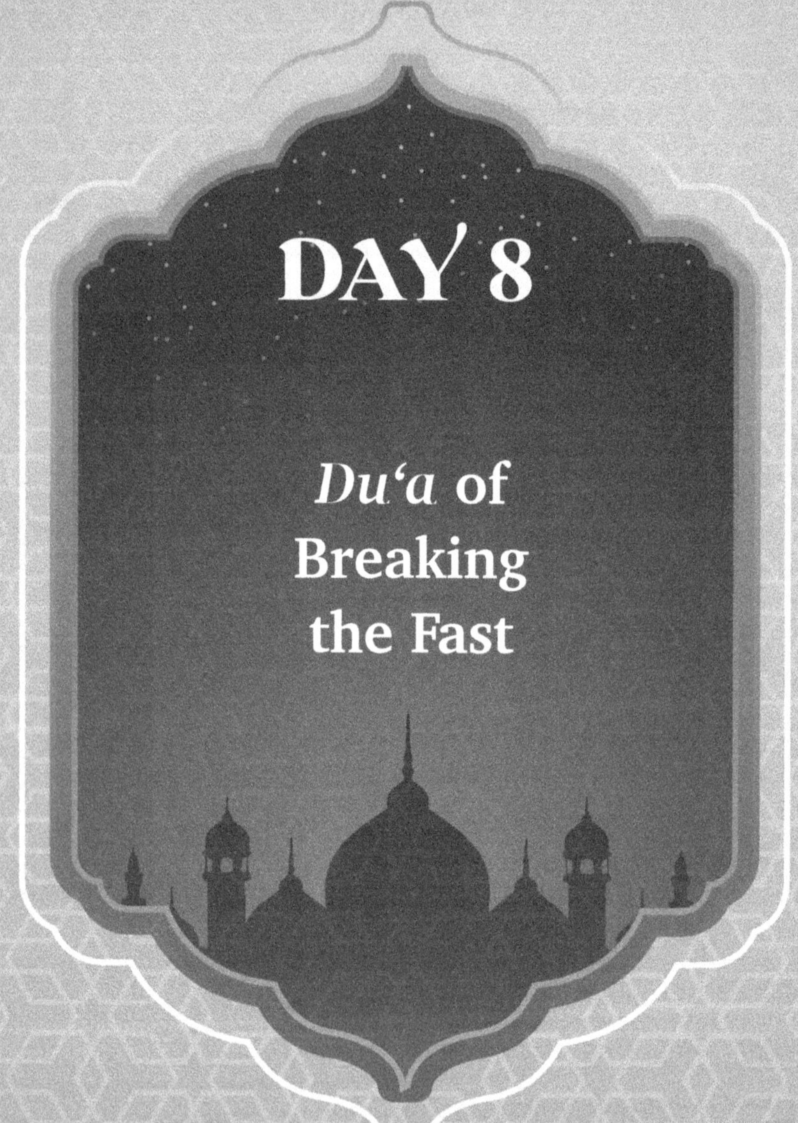
DAY 8
Du'a of
Breaking
the Fast

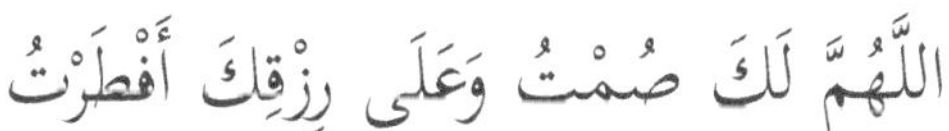

Allahumma laka sumtu wa 'ala rizqika aftartu

O Allah, for Thee I have fasted, and with Thy provision I have broken my fast. (*Sunan Abi Dawud* 2358)

There are a number of *du'a* that Prophet Muhammad ﷺ would recite at the time of breaking fast. One of the *du'a* that he would recite is:

وَابْتَلَّتِ الْعُرُوقُ وَثَبَتَ الأَجْرُ إِنْ شَاءَ اللَّهُ

...the arteries are moist, and the reward is sure, if Allah wills. (*Sunan Abi Dawud* 2357)

In this *du'a*, it illustrates that our veins have been irrigated, and that we have been nourished; therefore, we pray that Allah establishes this reward for us. May Allah سبحانه و تعالى accept our fasts.

The *du'a* we make do not necessarily have to be recited in Arabic. They can be made in our own mother tongue. Therefore, we should ask Allah سبحانه و تعالى during our moments of eating, particularly with the first *du'a* written above, "*Allahumma laka sumtu*; O Allah, to You I have fasted, *wa 'ala rizqika aftartu*; and upon Your *rizq* I break my fast."

This *du'a* is known as the *du'a* that was recited by Prophet Muhammad ﷺ in Ramadan, and is observed as one of the narrations that was reported by the *sahabah*. May Allah سبحانه و تعالى accept our fasts in the month of Ramadan. *Allahumma ameen*.

DAY 9
Full Belief and Submission to Allah

لَّآ إِلَـٰهَ إِلَّآ أَنتَ سُبۡحَـٰنَكَ إِنِّى كُنتُ مِنَ ٱلظَّـٰلِمِينَ ﴿٨٧﴾

La ilāha illa anta subhanaka inni kuntu minazzalimin

There is no god worthy of worship except You. Glory be to You! I have certainly done wrong. (*Surah Al Anbiya*, 21:87)

One of the greatest *du'a* that we can make is a *du'a* from the Qur'an. It is the *du'a* of Prophet Yunus عليه السلام . It is a *du'a* that is full of belief in Allah and the admission of one's guilt, and it is a *du'a* that saves one from all difficulties. Whenever we are facing difficulty or hardship in the decisions we make, or whenever we are facing our fears, we should remember the *du'a* of Yunus عليه السلام . It is the *du'a* of removing *karb*; that is, harm and difficulty.

The *du'a* of Prophet Yunus عليه السلام is quoted by Allah in *surah Al Anbiya*, "*La ilāha illa anta*; o Allah, there is no one that I worship but You, *subhanaka*; glorious, exalted, unblemished are You, o Allah, *inni kuntu minazzalimin*; I am the one who has wronged my own self, and I am the sinner before you, o Allah."

We should try our best to repeat this *du'a* as often as we can. *La ilāha illa anta, subhanaka inni kuntu minazzalimin. La ilāha illa anta, subhanaka inni kuntu minazzalimin.* It is one of the greatest *du'a* of protection from harm. May Allah سبحانه و تعالى accept our fasts on this blessed day of Ramadan.

DAY 10
Remembrance
of Allah

One of the greatest blessings of Allah سبحانه و تعالى can be attained with our recitation of *dhikr*. *Dhikr* is the remembrance of Allah. Allah سبحانه و تعالى says:

ٱذْكُرُوا۟ ٱللَّهَ ذِكْرًا كَثِيرًا ﴿٤١﴾

Always remember Allah often… (*Surah Al Ahzab*, 33:41)

We should recite Allah's name with intention. We include the word 'intention' because that is the way we can remember Allah whilst making our *dhikr*. There may be times where we find ourselves making *dhikr*, yet we could be reciting it in a very mindless manner. Acquire the remembrance of Allah with plentiness and abundance. The scholars of Islam say that that is one of the conditions of the remembrance of Allah; to do so incessantly and endlessly. We ought to understand that remembering Allah should always be a significant part of our life.

The *dhikr* of Allah سبحانه و تعالى is carried out with our heart, tongue, and through our actions. It is carried out with our heart by having sincerity with Allah سبحانه و تعالى. It is carried out with our tongue by mentioning the name of the One we love, fear, and hope for in His mercy, that is Allah سبحانه و تعالى . We should also use the invocations and formulas taught to us by Prophet Muhammad ﷺ, and proudly speak of our relationship with Allah, the Almighty. *Dhikr* is carried out with our actions by remembering Allah when we physically restrict ourselves from committing sins, and use our strength in a way that pleases Him.

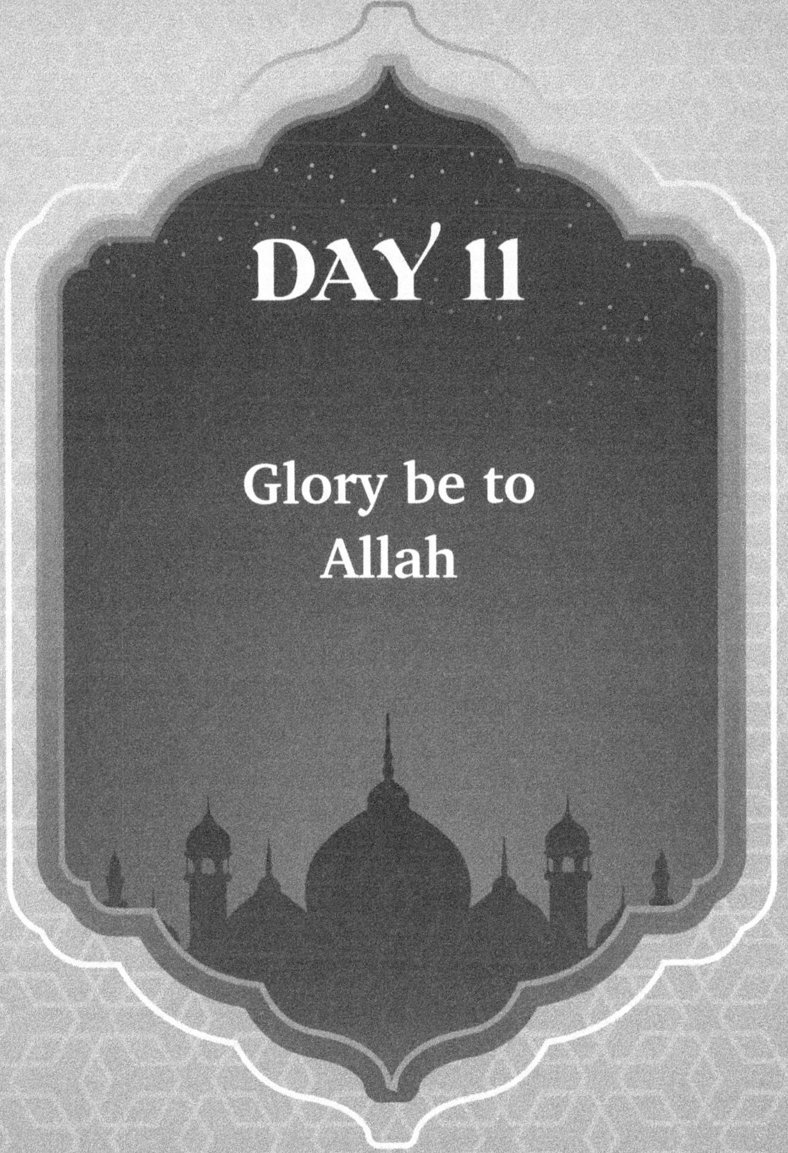

DAY 11

Glory be to Allah

سُبْحَانَ اللَّهِ

Subhanallah

Glory be to Allah

Subhanallah wa bihamdih

Glory be to Allah and all praise is due to Him

One of the significant ways of strengthening our relationship with Allah سبحانه و تعالى is through remembering Him; in other words, through the *dhikr* of Allah سبحانه و تعالى, which can be done in different ways. This reminds us of one of the greatest *dhikr*, which is to say '*subhanallah*' (سُبْحَانَ اللهِ), and '*subhanallah wa bihamdih*' (سُبْحَانَ اللهِ وَبِحَمْدِهِ).

Prophet Muhammad ﷺ said, "The one who says, "*Subhanallah, subhanallah wa bihamdih*," a hundred times in their day, their sins are forgiven even if they covered an ocean. (*Sahih Bukhari* 6405)

The saying '*subhanallah*' means we exalt Allah سبحانه و تعالى . We exalt the One who is unblemished without limits; the One who has no defects. May Allah سبحانه و تعالى place His grandeur in our hearts, and may Allah accept our fasts in this blessed Ramadan.

DAY 12
Removal of
Worries

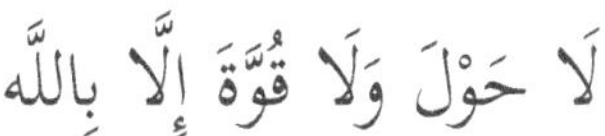

La hawla wa la quwwata illa billah

There is no power and strength, except with Allah. (*Sahih Muslim* 2704c)

This *dhikr* of Allah سبحانه و تعالى is very significant. One of the greatest *dhikr* of Allah سبحانه و تعالى is to say, "*La hawla wa la quwwata illa billah*." We have no power, might, authority, or ability, except that which is given to us by Allah.

This was one of the exclamations that many of the prophets of Allah made at a time of difficulty and stress. May Allah سبحانه و تعالى remove our worries, and may Allah make us from those who regularly send our devotions upon Him. Remember the statement '*la hawla wa la quwwata illa billah*.' It always helps to remember that we would not have the ability to turn or move our bodies or limbs; we would not have the power or authority to do the things that we do in our daily lives; we would not be able to do anything except that which is willed by Allah.

Therefore, anything that is taken from us or given to us; anything that we are increased with or decreased from; know that it is all by the might and power delegated to us by Allah سبحانه و تعالى .

DAY 13

Contentment and Satisfaction

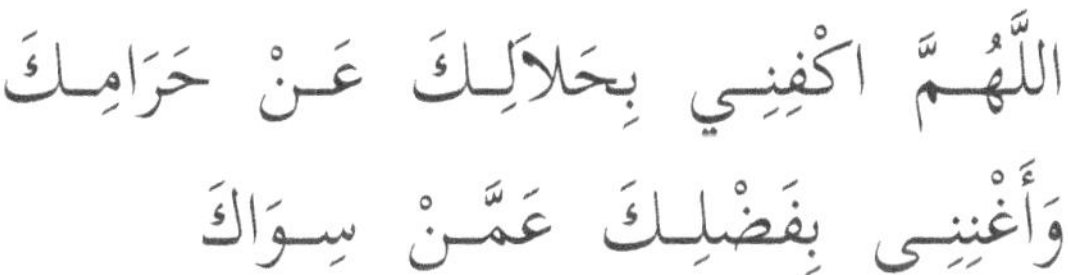

Allahummakfini bi halalika 'an haramik, wa aghnini bifadlika 'amman siwak

O Allah, suffice me with Your lawful against Your prohibited, and make me independent of all those besides You. (*Jami' at-Tirmidhi* 3563)

This is the *du'a* of Prophet Muhammad ﷺ, where he was known to recite, "*Allahummakfini bi halalika 'an haramik, wa aghnini bifadlika 'an man siwak. Allahumma*; o Allah, you are my Allah, *ikfini bi halalika 'an haramik*; make us worthy and wealthy through You, in a way that leads us away from *haram*."

"O Allah, *ikfina bi halalik*." Make us happy with the things that You have made *halal* that You have provided. Make the job that we have *halal*; despite it, perhaps, giving us a smaller *rizq* than we wish for. Make us feel enriched by it, so that it helps us to turn away from seeking the *haram*. "*Wa aghnina bifadlika 'amman siwak*." O Allah, make me enriched by relying on You, so that I will not need to rely on anyone else."

Allahumma; O Allah, *ikfina*; give us sufficiency, happiness, and enrichment, *bi halalik*; in what is *halal*, *'an haramik*; that turns us away from *haram*, *wa aghnina bifadlika*; and give us sufficiency and happiness in You, *'amman siwak*; through You, o Allah, so that we turn our hopes away in everyone else. *Allahumma ameen. Allahummakfina bi halalika 'an haramik, wa aghnina bifadlika 'amman siwak. Ameen.*

DAY 14

Concept of *Du‘a*

One of the greatest blessings of Allah سبحانه و تعالى is our opportunity to connect with Him, and that the opportunity is always available. The concept of *du'a* is a very important concept for us as Muslims. The word '*du'a*' implicitly means 'invitation', or 'to invite'. We acknowledge that it is Allah سبحانه و تعالى who is inviting us to request for His *barakah*; therefore, we are inviting the *barakah* of Allah into our life.

Allah سبحانه و تعالى seeks for us to invoke Him. The following *hadith* is *da'if*; however, the lesson behind it is very meaningful. Prophet Muhammad ﷺ said, "*Man lam yas alillah yaghdab 'alaih*," which carries the meaning, "The one who is not consistent in asking Allah for things, Allah is angry with them." (*Sunan Ibn Majah* 3827) Therefore, one of the things we should impress ourselves with in the blessed month of Ramadan is to be consistent with making *du'a*. Do not ever feel that we are asking for too much, or that we are asking for something that is too big, or too grand within our prayers. We are standing before the King of kings; therefore, do not ask for pennies. Ask for things that would reflect the majesty of the One you are asking from. May Allah accept all of our *du'a* in this blessed month of Ramadan.

DAY 15

Moments of *Du'a*

One of the important aspects of *du'a* is to know when it is most timely for our prayers to be accepted. One of the most *mustajab* timings for making *du'a* is during the blessed month of Ramadan. According to Prophet Muhammad ﷺ, there are two occasions in the day of fasting where our *du'a* is answered in Ramadan.

The first is during the time a person begins his fast, right until the moment he breaks his fast. (*Sunan Ibn Majah* 1752) Therefore, ensure that we make lots of *du'a* whilst fasting. The second is during the time a fasting person is about to break his fast. (*Jami' At-Tirmidhi* 3598) When we are busy preparing to eat, we should not also forget to busy ourselves with making *du'a* to Allah.

These occasions are seen as a valuable opportunity for us to fast, and have our efforts of making *du'a* complement our fasting efforts. With regards to the beauty of fasting and making *du'a*, Prophet Muhammad ﷺ reminds us of a verse in the Qur'an:

وَإِذَا سَأَلَكَ عِبَادِى عَنِّى فَإِنِّى قَرِيبٌ

﴿١٨٦﴾

When My servants ask you O Prophet about Me:
I am truly near. (*Surah Al Baqarah*, 2:186)

May Allah سبحانه و تعالى accept all of our *du'a* in the month of Ramadan. *Allahumma ameen.*

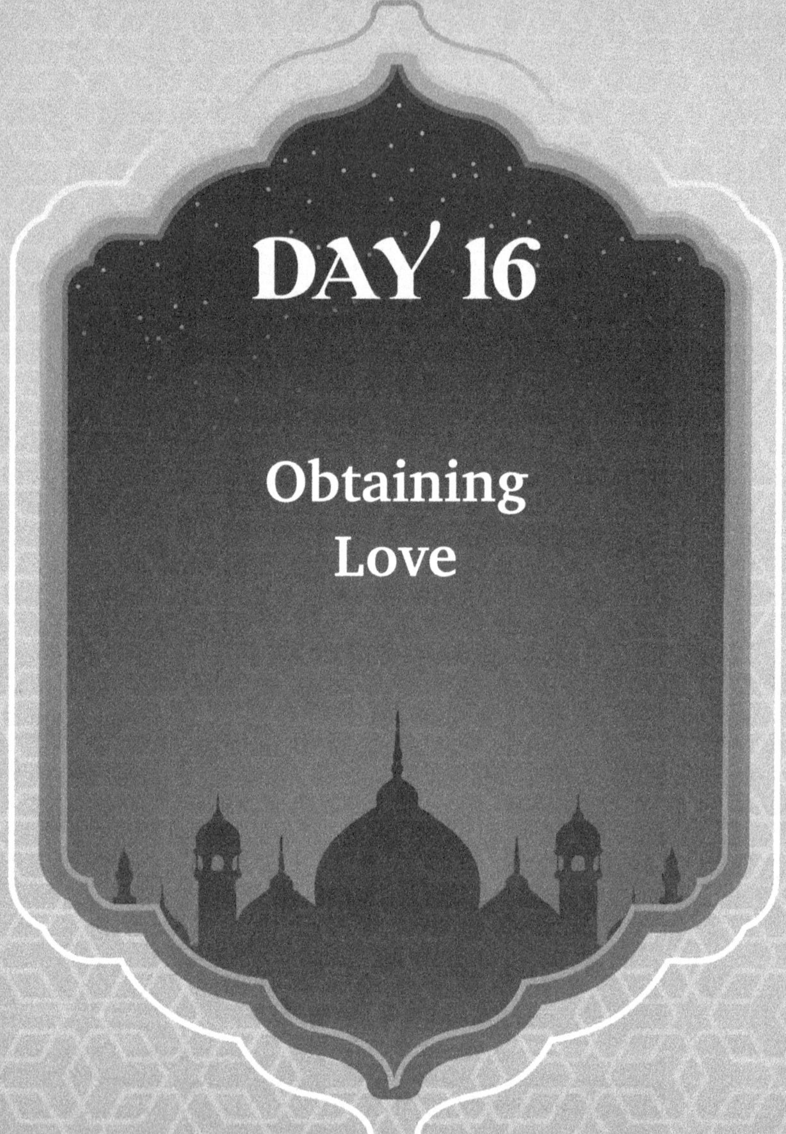

DAY 16

Obtaining Love

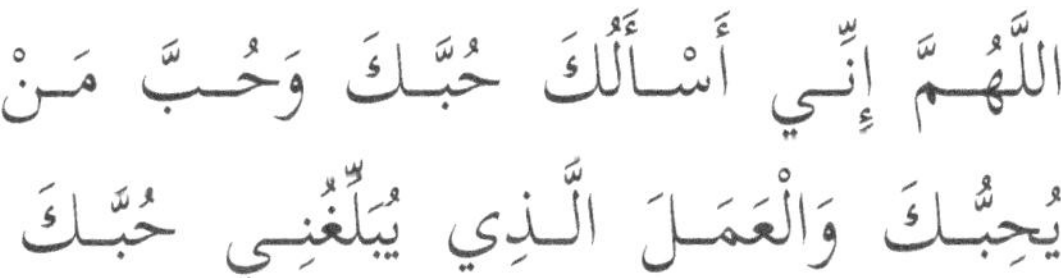

Allahumma inni as'aluka hubbak, wa hubba man yuhibbuk, wal amal alladhi yuballighuni hubbak

O Allah, indeed, I ask You for Your love, and the love of those who love You, and for the action that will cause me to attain Your love... (*Jami' at-Tirmidhi* 3490)

One of the secrets of the month of Ramadan is that it is a fruitful time for us to increase our love towards Allah and other creations of Allah. If we find ourselves struggling to love or care other people outside the month of Ramadan, then Ramadan is a great month to seek compassion within ourselves. As Muslims striving to become the best versions of ourselves, we hope to find love in Allah, Prophet Muhammad ﷺ, the communities that we live in, our children, our family, even our enemies, and many more other types of people. Each of these relationships withhold a different kind of love that we seek. Therefore, we should ask Allah سبحانه و تعالى to make us among those who love one another. In seeking this love, Prophet Muhammad ﷺ used to make this *du'a*.

"*Allahumma inni as'aluka hubbak, wa hubba man yuhibbuk, wal amal alladhi yuballighuni hubbak*. O Allah, we ask You for Your love, the love of those who love You, and the love of the deeds that makes us endeared and loved by You." May Allah سبحانه و تعالى accept our fasts on this blessed day of Ramadan. *Ameen*.

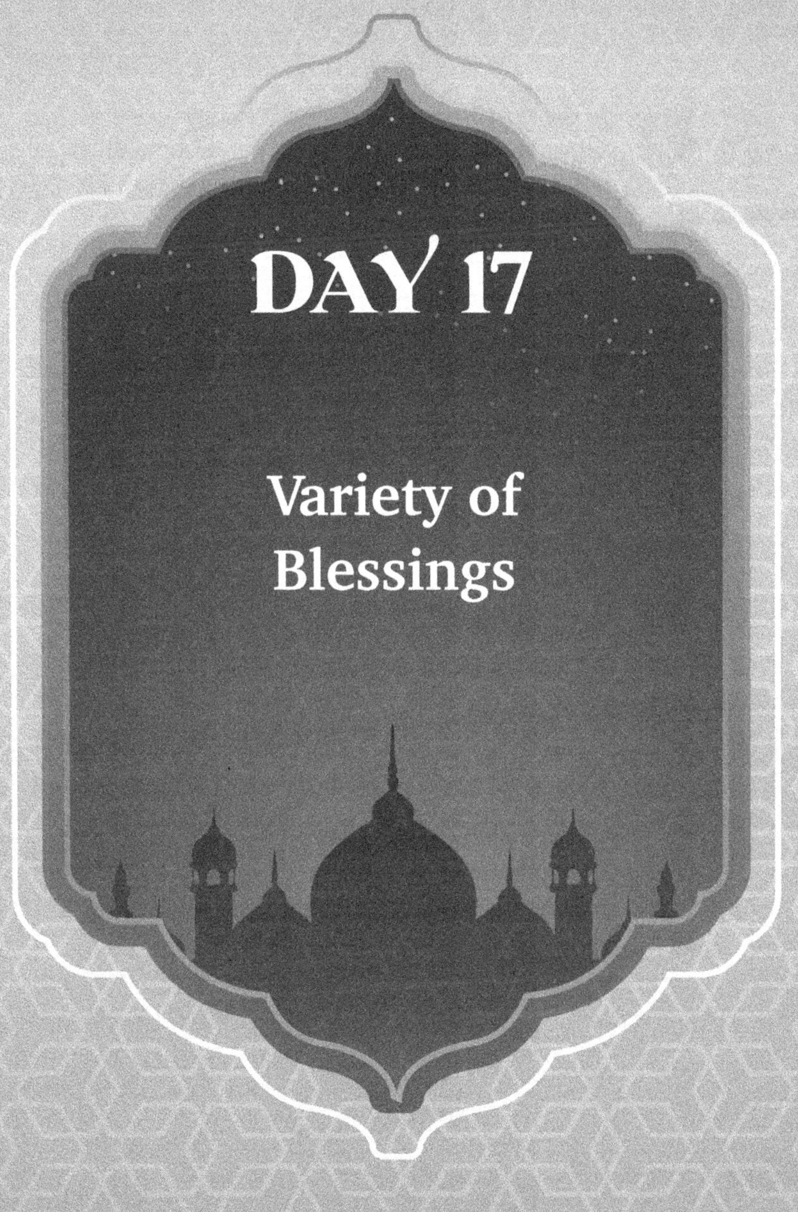

DAY 17

Variety of Blessings

One of the ways that we hear Prophet Muhammad ﷺ describe the month of Ramadan is that the month is observed as a *barakah*. Prophet Muhammad ﷺ said:

أَتَاكُمْ رَمَضَانُ شَهْرٌ مُبَارَكٌ

> There has come to you Ramadan, a blessed month.(*Sunan an-Nasa'i* 2106)

'*Barakah*' means three things. First, it means when Allah سبحانه و تعالى is giving us something that we do not yet have. Therefore, we should ask Allah for anything and everything that we need. Second, it means when Allah protects something that we have, but may have been lost if Allah did not safeguard it for us. Therefore, we should ask Allah سبحانه و تعالى to protect our health, wealth, family, and loved ones. Third, it means when Allah سبحانه و تعالى gives us something that we have been asking for, yet did not think we could ever achieve. For example, we dream of achieving something that seems a little beyond reach. We do not know how it would ever happen, yet Allah fulfils our wish in a way or from a place that we did not expect.

Those are the three types of *barakah* that can be found in the month of Ramadan. May Allah سبحانه و تعالى allow us to achieve these *barakah* in all aspects through our fasts. *Wa sallillahumma wa sallim wa zid wa barik 'ala sayyidina wa nabiyyina Muhammad* ﷺ.

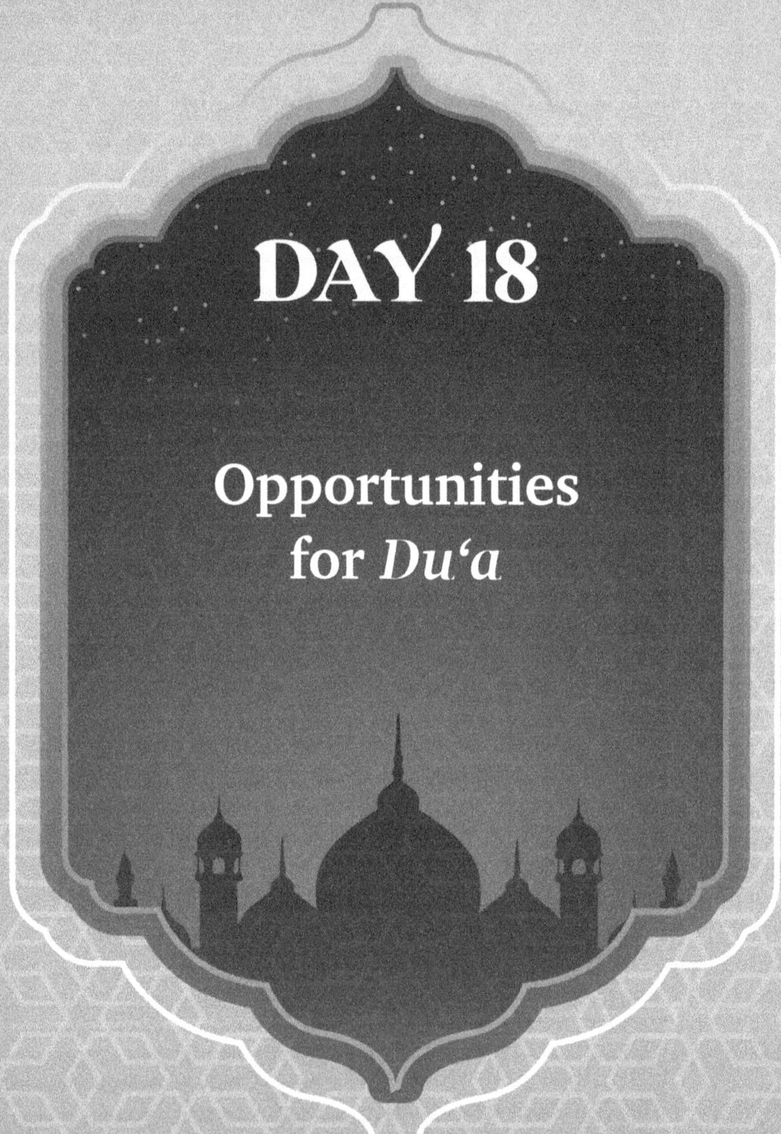

DAY 18

Opportunities for *Du'a*

One of the greatest blessings of Allah سبحانه و تعالى in the month of Ramadan is that it is a valuable time for our *du'a* to be answered. This topic was previously mentioned in the earlier chapters. However, another important aspect to know about making *du'a* is that there are other valuable opportunities that can be found in our day to day life where our *du'a* could also be readily accepted.

One of the *mustajab* timings for making *du'a* is between the *adhan* and the *iqamah* of any prayer. Whenever we hear the *adhan*, right until the *iqamah* is being called; the time between the two callings, we should make *du'a* to Allah to ask for anything we wish for. Prophet Muhammad ﷺ said that the likelihood of our *du'a* being answered is similar to when we are in a state of *sujud*. Therefore, we should also make *du'a* and ask Allah to fulfil our wishes during the prostrations in our prayers. (*Sunan an-Nasa'i* 1137)

Another cherished opportunity for Allah to accept our *du'a* is after performing a righteous deed. Anas ibn Malik رضي الله عنه used to make supplications with his family upon the completion of their Qur'an recitation. (*Al-Darimi* 3517) Therefore, whenever we finish reciting the Qur'an, invoke Allah and make *du'a* to mark the end of the recitation. These are some of the treasured opportunities for us to make *du'a* to Allah in this blessed month of Ramadan.

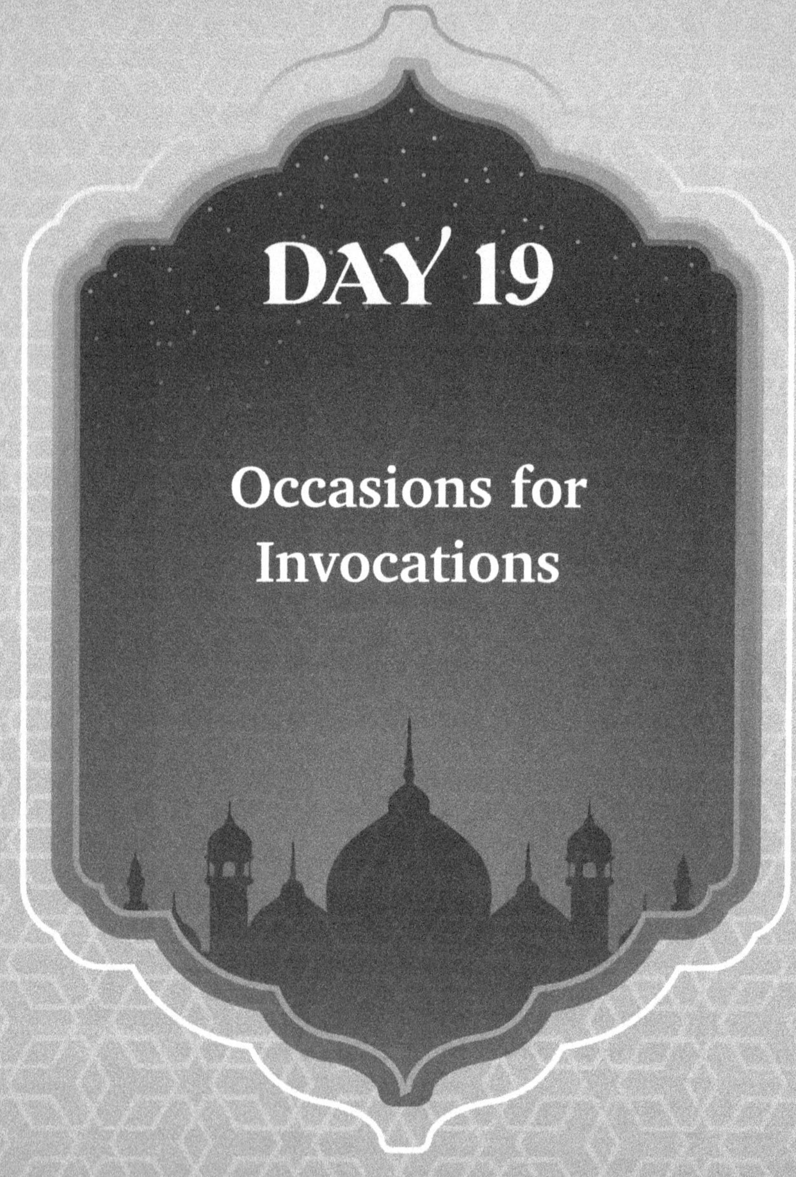

DAY 19

Occasions for Invocations

Making *du'a* is a very important act in the month of Ramadan, and there are a number of other occasions to when our *du'a* is more likely to be answered. One of them is during the depths of the night. Prophet Muhammad ﷺ says that in the third part of the night, Allah descends to the Heavens. In this context, the notion of Allah descending should only be understood as that which is befitting to the majesty of Allah سبحانه و تعالى, and is beyond our comprehension.

During this time, Allah سبحانه و تعالى asks the angels, "Who has left their sleep and is awake to ask Me for things that I shall give him? Who is awake to seek My forgiveness, so that I shall forgive him?" As an effort to grab this opportunity in the blessed month of Ramadan, we should make it a habit to wake up, not only for *suhoor* and *Fajr* prayer; however, to wake up a little bit earlier in order to make voluntary prayers and *du'a* to Allah during this precious time.

Should we manage to wake up earlier than usual and able to make *munaja* to Allah in the blessed month of Ramadan; turning to Him to fulfil our needs and seeking for His forgiveness, it is vouched by Prophet Muhammad ﷺ that our prayers shall be heard and answered by Allah سبحانه و تعالى . May Allah accept our *du'a*, as well as our fasts in the month of Ramadan. *Allahumma ameen*.

DAY 20

Du'a on the Night of Decree

اللَّهُمَّ إِنَّكَ عَفُوٌّ كَرِيمٌ تُحِبُّ الْعَفْوَ فَاعْفُ عَنِّي

Allahumma innaka 'afuwun karim tuhibbul 'afuwa fa'afu 'anni

O Allah, indeed You are the Pardoner, and You love to pardon, so pardon me. (*Jami' at-Tirmidhi* 3513)

One of the greatest *du'a* that would be made by Prophet Muhammad ﷺ, particularly during the last ten nights of Ramadan, as an effort to seek for the night of *Lailatul Qadr*, was the *du'a* he taught his wife, A'isha رضي الله عنه . A'isha رضي الله عنه asked, "If I encounter the night of *Lailatul Qadr*, what *du'a* should I make?" Prophet Muhammad ﷺ then taught her this *du'a*.

"*Allahumma*; o my Lord, Allah, You are my Allah, *innaka*; You alone, *'afuwwun*; pardon, expiate, forgive, wipe away my sins, *tuhibbul 'afwa*; You love to wipe away the sins of Your servants, to pardon the sins, to overlook our mistakes, *fa'fu'anni*; so pardon me, expiate my sins, remove my sins from my record, o Allah." *Allahumma innaka 'afuwwun karim tuhibbul 'afwa fa'fu'anni.*

May Allah make us among those whose sins are erased, and among those who are blessed with standing before Allah on the night of *Lailatul Qadr* in a state of invoking Him with this *du'a* and have our sins expiated. *Wa sallillahumma wa sallim wa zid wa barik 'ala sayyidina Muhammad.*

DAY 21

Making *Du'a* for Others

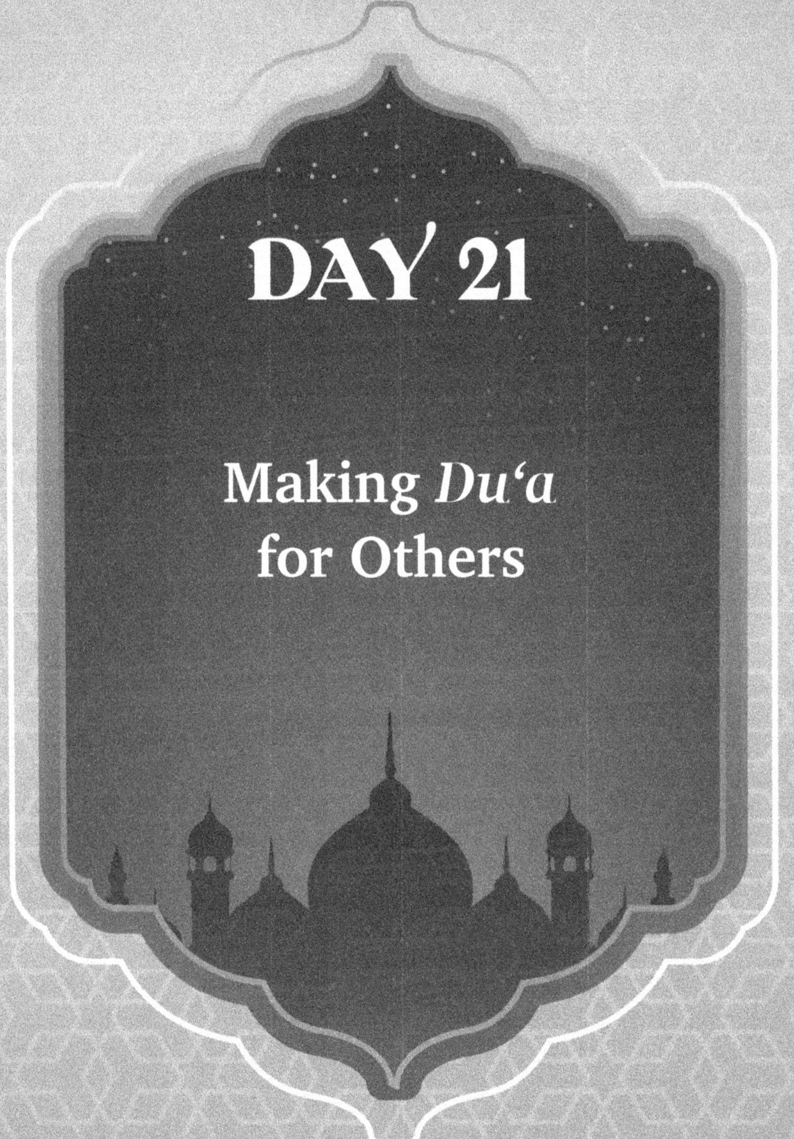

Making *du'a* in the month of Ramadan is a significant act to perform as we have learned, and one of the best *du'a* to make is a *du'a* for ourself and our family.

One of the *sunnah* of Prophet Muhammad ﷺ in making *du'a* is not to make it merely unilateral, or not to make *du'a* simply for ourselves. In fact, Prophet Muhammad ﷺ said, "The one who makes *du'a* for their brother, friend, or someone they love; without the knowledge that *du'a* has been made for them, is answered by Allah, who sends an angel and the angel says, '*Ameen*, and to you the same goodness you ask for that person.'" (*Sahih Muslim* 2732a & 2732b)

Therefore, one of the ways that we can be given great blessings by Allah سبحانه و تعالى for ourselves is to be generous with our *du'a*. When we increase our love for others, it simultaneously increases Allah's love for us. May Allah accept our *du'a* for ourselves and others, and make it a reflection of *barakah* in our life. *Allahumma ameen. Wa sallillahumma wa sallim wa zid wa barik 'ala sayyidina Muhammad.*

DAY 22

Helping the Orphans

One of the acts that is important for us to try and carry out before Ramadan departs is for us to help the orphans. Allah سبحانه و تعالى says in the Qur'an:

فَأَمَّا ٱلْيَتِيمَ فَلَا تَقْهَرْ ﴿٩﴾

So do not oppress the orphan. (*Surah Ad Dhuha*, 93:9)

We should never turn away, or despise an orphan, or turn away the opportunity to help an orphan. Prophet Muhammad ﷺ himself was an orphan. In this blessed month of Ramadan, ensure that a part of our *sadaqah* and charity goes to the orphans. Prophet Muhammad ﷺ said:

كَافِلُ الْيَتِيمِ لَهُ أَوْ لِغَيْرِهِ أَنَا وَهُوَ كَهَاتَيْنِ فِي الْجَنَّةِ

"The one who looks after an orphan whether he is his relative or not, he and I would be together in Paradise like this," and Malik explained it with the gesture of drawing his index finger and middle finger closely together. (*Sahih Muslim* 2983)

It may be implied that Prophet Muhammad ﷺ is demonstrating the elevated status of those who assist orphans. Helping fellow orphans may seem like a small act of deed; however, it is through these little changes between elevations that we increase our status and become closer to Prophet Muhammad ﷺ. May Allah open our hearts to help the orphans of our communities, as well as other orphans who may live further away from us, yet still require our help. *Wa sallillahumma wa sallim wa zid wa barik 'ala sayyidina wa nabiyyina Muhammad.*

DAY 23

Attaining *Lailatul Qadr*

Encountering the night of *Lailatul Qadr* is one of the greatest aspirations that we all have as Muslims. Based on the Qur'an and *hadith,* we learn that there are signs we can identify in the day and night to know of its presence. It is within the last ten nights that one can learn to identify the signs of *Lailatul Qadr*; the scarcer portion of Ramadan.

Although we may be unable to foresee exactly when *Lailatul Qadr* will occur, fellow *ulama'* tell us that it should not be one particular night that we should be seeking; however, we ought to seek it every night through the last ten nights of Ramadan. In other words, we should perform the best of our *'ibada*h throughout the entire, final ten nights. The closer we reach towards the final ten nights of Ramadan, the more effort we should put into performing our deeds. When we reach the 18th, or the 19th night of Ramadan; we should strive to make extra effort. There is no loss whatsoever in our efforts to perform the best we can in the month of Ramadan.

As he enters the final ten nights of Ramadan, Prophet Muhammad ﷺ would double; sometimes, quadruple, his efforts in his *'ibadah*. An excellent way to attain *Lailatul Qadr* as we get through the last ten nights is to be in a state of *i'tikaf*. Even if it is just for one day, or one hour, make intention to perform *i'tikaf* as we seclude ourselves in worship at the *masjid*, as a temporary rest from our affairs of this worldly life.

This is a beautiful blessing from Allah سبحانه و تعالى . May He bless us with *Lailatul Qadr*, a month that is worth a thousand months. *Allahumma ameen*. May Allah bless us with it, *ajma'in*.

DAY 24
Forgiving
Others

One of the things that we would see in every *masjid* around the world is a Muslim putting his hands up, praying to Allah saying, "*Allahummarhamna, Allahummaghfirlana*," which means, "O Allah, forgive us. O Allah, have mercy upon us. *Allahumma inni tubtu ilaik*; which means, "O Allah, I ask You to accept my repentance."

However, at times, we observe many of the same people, who ask for forgiveness for their sins with Allah, are unwilling to forgive others. They forget the words of Prophet Muhammad ﷺ:

الرَّاحِمُونَ يَرْحَمُهُمُ الرَّحْمَنُ ارْحَمُوا أَهْلَ الأَرْضِ يَرْحَمْكُمْ مَنْ فِي السَّمَاءِ

> The compassionate One has mercy on those who are merciful. If you show mercy to those who are on the earth, He, Who is in the Heavens, will show mercy to you. (*Sunan Abi Dawud* 4941)

Arrahimuna yarhamhum ar-rahman. It is only those who are merciful who Allah will show mercy. *Irhamu ahlal ardhi yarhamkum man fissama'*. Should we be able to show mercy and compassion to those who live among us, the One above the Heaven will show compassion to us. If we are unwilling to accept the forgiveness and pardon of other people over the mistakes they may have committed with us, how could we ask from the One who is Most Forgiving to forgive us? We should ensure that our hearts are open to forgive others as much as we would wish to be forgiven.

In this blessed month of Ramadan, we should look past our differences, and be willing to accept the amends that people put forward to us. May Allah سبحانه و تعالى remove our pride and ego, and increase goodness in us to forgive others in order to earn His forgiveness as well. *Allahumma ameen.*

DAY 25

Paying *Zakat al-Fitr*

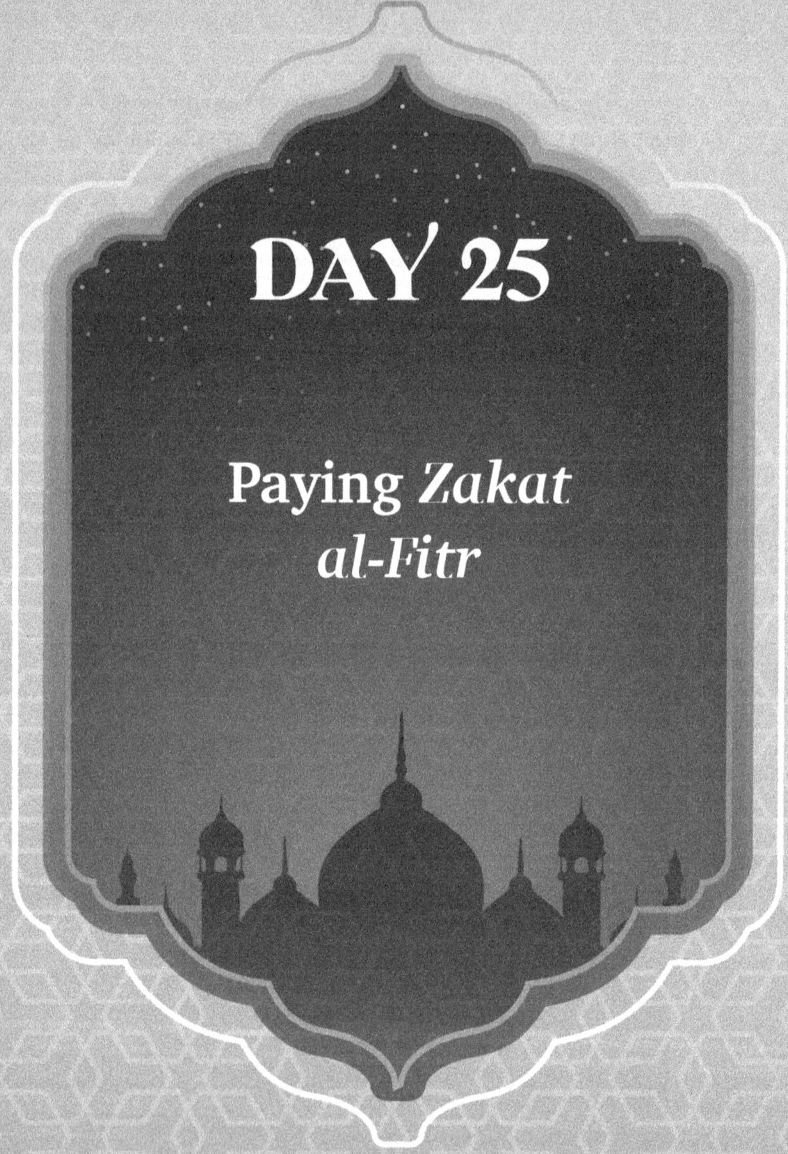

As the month of Ramadan is approaching its end, we should begin to think about performing our *zakat al-Fitr*. *Zakat al-Fitr* is the amount of food, or its equivalent in wealth, that we ought to contribute to our Muslim communities. By contributing to the *zakat al-Fitr*, we can try to ensure as many people within the Muslim communities, be it those within our local context or those living further away from us, have something to eat on *Eid al-Fitr*, the first day of *Shawwal*. It is also helpful to remember that *zakat al-Fitr* is not tied to the validity of our fast in Ramadan.

We should not confuse *zakat al-Fitr* as a form of tax we pay to ensure the mistakes we may have committed in Ramadan are forgiven, as that is not the case. We pray that deeds we carry out in Ramadan shall be accepted, *inshaa Allah*; however, *zakat al-Fitr* is observed as a form of right that Allah has determined for us to fulfil towards those who are less fortunate than ourselves. Therefore, who has to pay *zakat al-Fitr*? All of the people who are fathers. Those who carry the social responsibility of being a father, he should pay *zakat al-Fitr* to his wife, mother, brother, sister, and infants; such as babies and toddlers who still need to be held and suckled.

The amount of *zakat al-Fitr* that a person has to pay is the amount of an honest meal that you and I would consume and would be content with. Therefore, we should observe the amount of *zakat al-Fitr* that has been accounted by the respective community and *masjid*. We must ensure that *zakat al-Fitr* is paid before the *Eid al-Fitr* prayer. It is also permissible to perform it one or two days before the first day of Eid. However, we are highly discouraged to wait until the first day of Eid to do so. We ought to be determined to pay it earlier on to allow other unfortunate Muslims around us to be sufficed and happy on the day of Eid in the same way as Allah has blessed it for us. May Allah accept our fast, and make us among those who are always fortunate. *Allahumma ameen.*

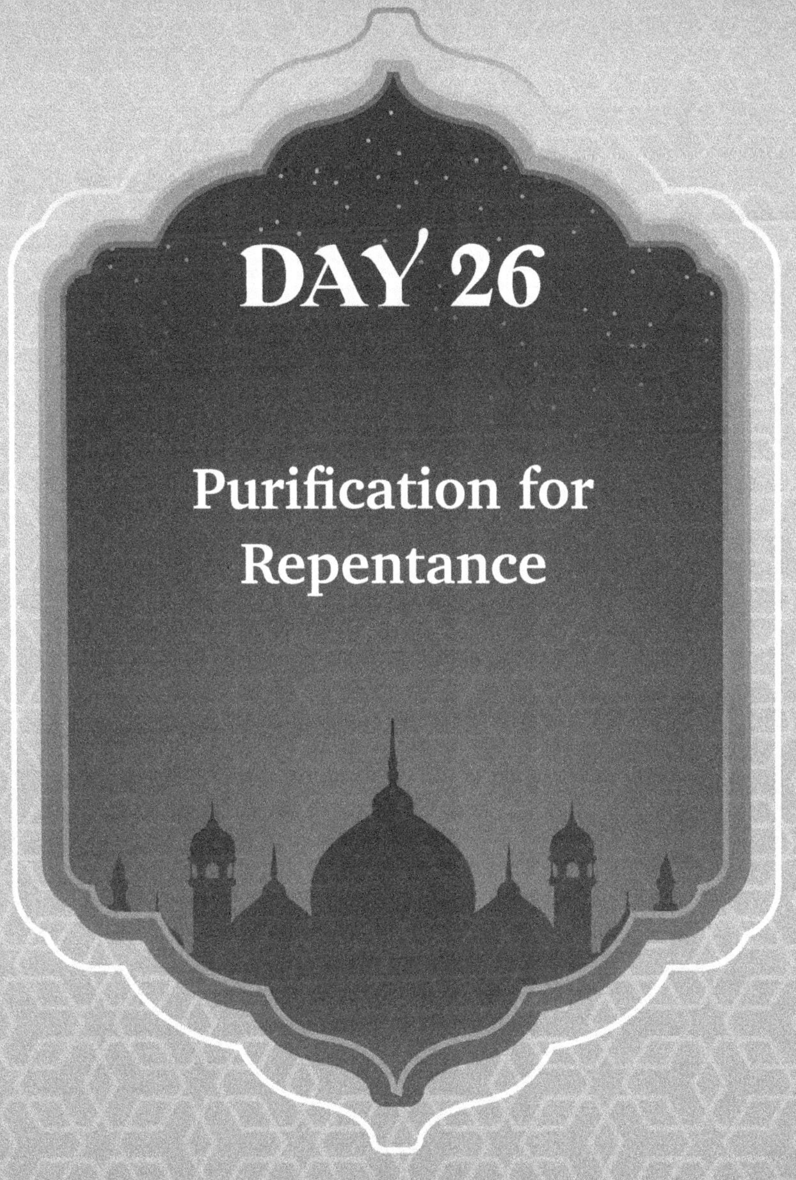
DAY 26
Purification for
Repentance

Love is one of the greatest outcomes of the month of Ramadan, especially seeking love from our Lord, Allah سبحانه و تعالى . One of the greatest ways to achieve Allah's love is to do the things that we know He loves. Allah سبحانه و تعالى tells us in the Qur'an:

إِنَّ ٱللَّهَ يُحِبُّ ٱلتَّوَّٰبِينَ وَيُحِبُّ ٱلْمُتَطَهِّرِينَ ﴿٢٢٢﴾

Surely Allah loves those who always turn to Him in repentance and those who purify themselves. (*Surah Al Baqarah*, 2:222)

Allah loves those who purify themselves and seek to be pure. Purification, or *taharah*, is done in three ways. First, there is the purification of the heart. This is called *tazkiyah*. *Tazkiyah* is to cleanse our heart of various ailments that may have gathered, such as anger, wrath, jealousy, or wickedness. A person who aims to attain *tazkiyah* is a person who tries to cleanse his heart from such ailments.

Second is *taharah*, which is a physical form of purification. Examples may include the *taharah* of our clothing, actions, or intentions. Third is also *taharah*;

however, the *taharah* of our tongues and minds. For example, this may include the things that we hear, say, see, and do. These three levels of purification can help us to ascend in seeking a greater kind of nearness to Allah سبحانه و تعالى.

It is interesting to learn that the three levels of purification can be achieved through the acts that we carry out in the month of Ramadan. Our body seeks *taharah* during this time; we try our best to keep our tongue and actions clean whilst we are fasting, and we try to be the person who cleanses his heart through the many *'ibadah* we practice in Ramadan. May Allah make us among those who are accepting of His love, and those who reciprocate the love of Allah back towards Himself and other people through our actions and dealings with them. *Allahumma ameen.*

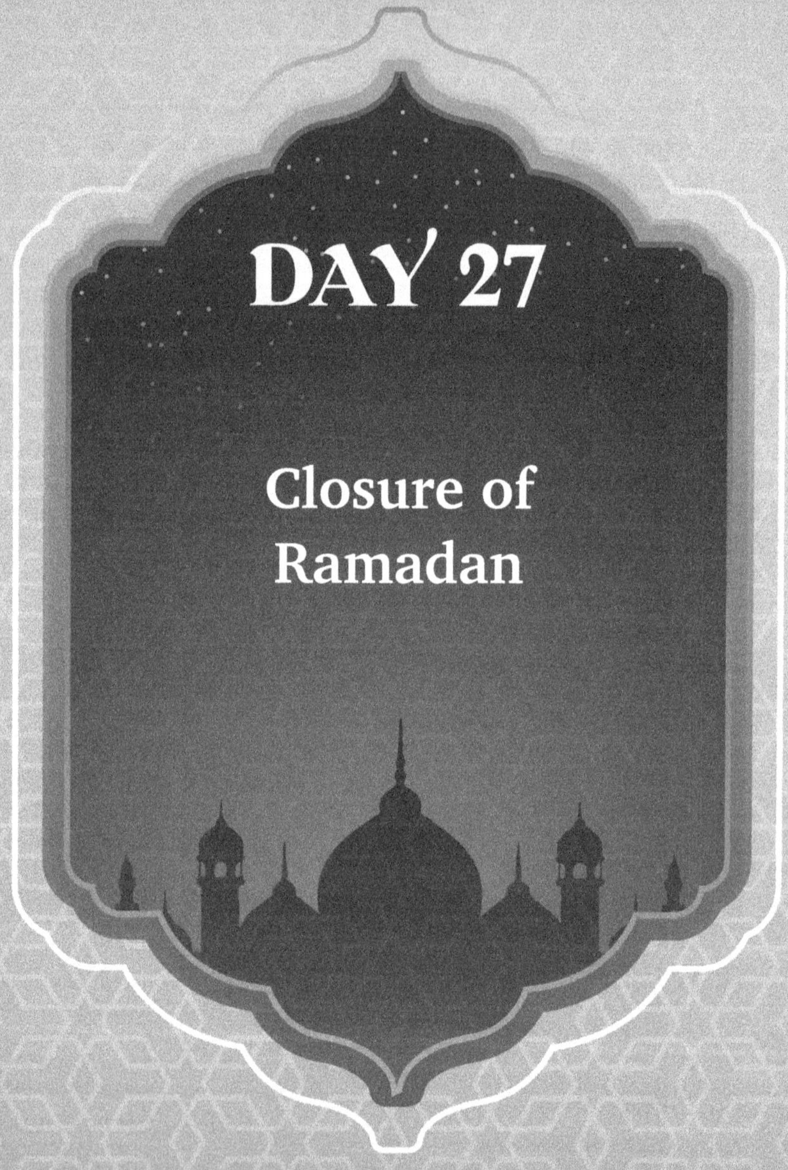

DAY 27

Closure of Ramadan

The month of Ramadan is coming to a close. As we prepare for Eid, it is important for us to know that it is an occasion that we have been blessed with. The *shaytan* will try to make us feel as though we have not done enough. However, we must know that it is Allah who has allowed us to meet the month of Ramadan, live through the month of Ramadan, stand before Him in Ramadan, fast for Him; in some cases, He may have given us expiation for not being able to fast, and that Allah سبحانه و تعالى has shown us favour, love and mercy.

As positive Muslims, it is helpful to have hope, and to know that Allah has accepted us and our deeds in this month of Ramadan. Do not be among those who despair in the mercy of Allah. Know that through our sincere efforts, we shall be among those who are forgiven. We have fasted, prayed, and made *du'a* to Allah. May Allah سبحانه و تعالى seal His favour upon us, and seal the blessed month of Ramadan with His acceptance. May Allah make us among those who are joyful on the day of Eid. *Allahumma ameen.*

DAY 28

Loving Others

Seeking Allah سبحانه و تعالى in the month of Ramadan is beyond merely fasting, and enduring our hunger and thirst. To seek Allah also includes building and improving our relationships with other people. One of the most powerful *hadith* of Prophet Muhammad ﷺ is one that speaks about earning Allah's love, and earning it through our love towards others.

My love is obliged (*Riyadh as-Salihin* 382)

Wajabat mahabbati. Allah vows that it is an obligation to receive His love for those who love other people. May Allah make us among those who are capable of portraying this compassion and *rahmah* towards others. We pray that would be able to love even those who have committed mistakes, or have been offensive, towards us or other people because it could be because of our inability to love such people that we are deprived of Allah's love towards us. May Allah سبحانه و تعالى protect us from the inability to love.

Do you not love to be forgiven by Allah? (*Surah An Nur*, 24:22)

We should ask ourselves, “Do we seek Allah سبحانه و تعالى to be as forgiving towards us?” The answer should undoubtedly be, “Yes.” This begins with having compassion within ourselves, and the ability to forgive others. May Allah سبحانه و تعالى increase our love and compassion for other people in this blessed month, so that we are able to earn Allah’s love, mercy, and compassion therein.

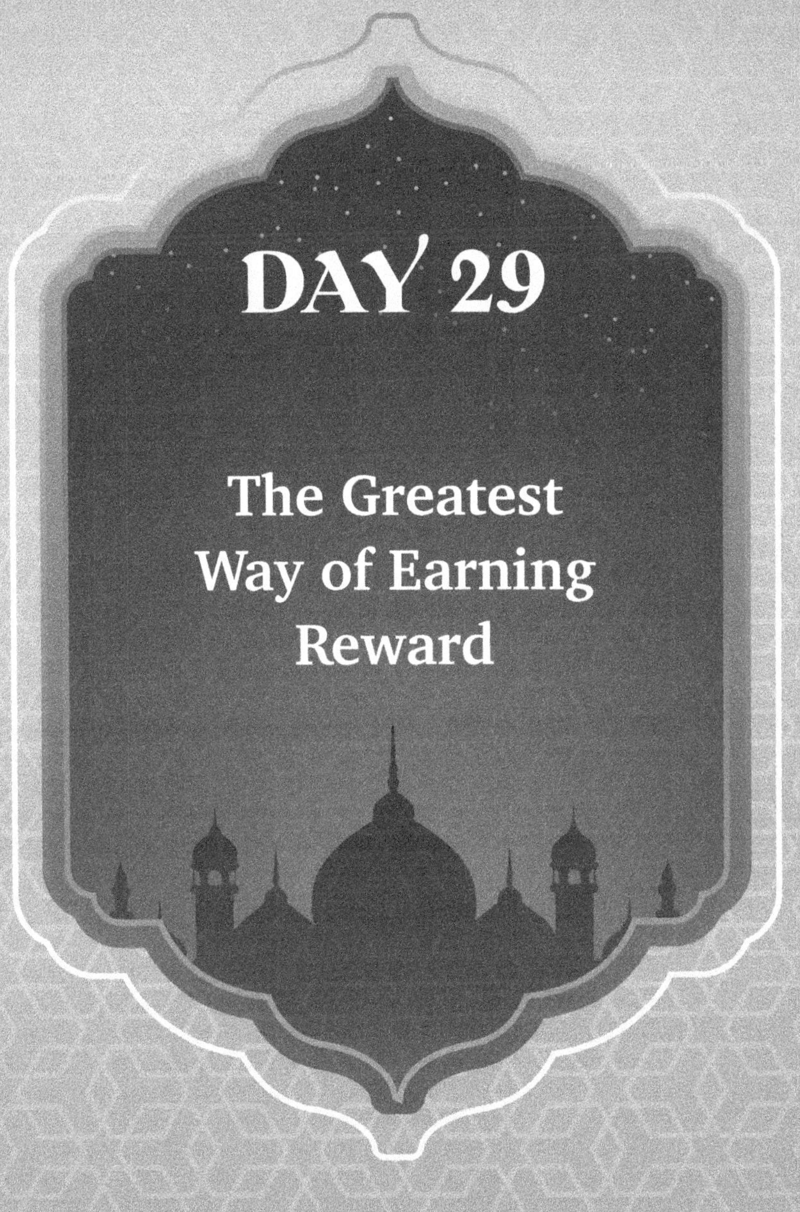

DAY 29

The Greatest Way of Earning Reward

سُبْحَانَ اللَّهِ وَبِحَمْدِهِ، سُبْحَانَ اللَّهِ الْعَظِيمِ

Subhan Allahi wa bihamdihi; Subhan Allahil 'Azim,

Allah is free from imperfection and all praise is due to Him; Allah is free from imperfection, the Greatest. (*Sahih Bukhari* 6682)

This *du'a* is the final recorded *hadith* by Imam Bukhari in his *sahih* collection of *hadith*. It has been narrated by Abu Hurairah رضي الله عنه . It is a *hadith* that many of us may be familiar with; therefore, let us ensure we know of this *dhikr* and *du'a*. This *dhikr* is powerful, and is one that fills the scale on the Day of Judgement with reward. The Prophet ﷺ was heard to have said, and this is narrated by many of the books and chains of collection, "There are two statements that are beloved to the Merciful, Allah سبحانه و تعالى . They are very light on the tongue, but heavy on the scales of the Day of Judgement."

سُبْحَانَ اللَّهِ وَبِحَمْدِهِ، سُبْحَانَ اللَّهِ الْعَظِيمِ

These are the two statements that are beloved to Allah, the Lord of Mercy. One of the *du'a* that we have studied is when we ask Allah سبحانه و تعالى , "O Allah, we ask You for Your love, and the love of those who love You, and the love of the deeds that earn Your love." This is one of those deeds. These two statements are beloved to Allah. Each of them is singularly loved by Allah. However, when we put the two statements together, they are even more loved and blessed by Allah.

Therefore, these statements on their own; for example, *Subhan Allah wa bihamdi* is a blessing on its own. The *dhikr 'Subhan Allah wa bihamdi'* is contained in many different hadith and *du'a* as mentioned by Prophet Muhammad ﷺ. It is the *du'a* we say in our *sujud*, "*Subhan Allahi wa bihamdi.*" In an authentic *hadith* in Bukhari and Muslim, the Prophet ﷺ said that the one who says this *dhikr* a hundred times in their day, their sins are forgiven even if they were to envelope and cover the oceans. The other *dhikr*, *'Subhanallahil 'azim'*, is what we say in our *ruku'*. This is the natural habit of a believer; to be excessive and consistent in praising Allah سبحانه و تعالى with these two particular *du'a*.

Why are these *dhikr* so significant? Both of them begins with *'subhan'*. The word *'subhan'*, such as the *dhikr 'Subhan Allah'*, comes from *sa-ba-ha*, which means 'infinite process', or something which we do not know its limit. Something that we cannot estimate with its ending or its beginning. Limitless is Your Glory, O Allah. Nothing could ever take away Your Completeness, O Allah. There is no change to Your Grandeur, Your Majesty, or Your Magnificence, O Allah. There is nothing that alters Your *Rahmah*, O Allah. There is nothing that changes the greatest qualities of Allah. *Subhan Allah*. Therefore, we say this *dhikr* as an exclamation towards something beautiful, or also something repugnant.

When we hear people claim that Allah has an offspring, or a shared accomplice in this world, we ought to say, "*Subhan Allah.*" How can anyone say this? It is not fit for the Majestic, *Ar-Rahman*, the Lord of Mercy, to beget a child. *Subhan Allah*, glorified is His Limitlessness; He is beyond this need or any need, and all praises are due to Him.The *'hamd'* of Allah applies to two things; it means that we elevate Allah, and we limit it from anyone or anything other than Him. Therefore, we make this *hamd* and praise Allah in a way that nothing else is deserving of; in a way that nothing else is worshipped.

This is the secret behind this recitation in our *sujud*, as we will never make *sujud* to anything or anyone but

Allah. He is the only One worthy of our servitude and enslavement. We approach the end of our prayer by claiming and attesting our statement, conviction, and belief that Allah is Al-'Azim. He is Greater than all things. He is Mightier than all things. Dear brother and sister; whatever problems we may have, Allah is there. Whatever hardship we face, Allah is there. The *du'a* above is light upon the tongue, but heavy on the scales of the Day of Judgement.

In the last chapter of his collection, Imam Bukhari mentions about *tawhid*; the uniqueness of Allah in our worship as being the only One who is Eternal. Imam Bukhari narrated this *hadith* because it was the most perfect way to end a book of *hadith* with the greatest way of earning reward, that is to ask Allah through this *dhikr*. In addition, it also shows us the conviction that we have towards our belief that we will be questioned about how we have lived. Our deeds will be weighed. If we know that our good deeds are light due to particular reasons, and we want to increase the weight of our good deeds, we should do so by saying these simple statements. Seal this Ramadan series of therapy, which we pray Allah will accept from us all, by understanding this point.

The simplest statements are the ones that will earn us the greatest rewards from Allah. The greatest *ayat* from the Qur'an is *ayatul-kursi*. It protects us from harm. This was the topic that we began with, the last two verses from *surah Al-Baqarah*. Consider that the simplest of deeds will earn us the greatest of rewards and make this testament to it. May Allah make us worthy of our place with Him in a high standing in Jannah.

May Allah make our deeds a testament for us that Allah will create a love for them. May Allah grant us love in this life, and grant us His greatest love on the Day of Judgement, and enjoins us together because of our love for Him, and our love for His *nabi* ﷺ in the highest level of Paradise, *Al-Firdaus*, within the circles of the prophets, the martyrs, the righteous, and the verifiers of truths. *Allahumma āmīn*. May Allah سبحانه و تعالى elevate our names. May we always mention Allah so that He shall mention us. May we remember Allah and make *du'a* to Him outside of the month of Ramadan the way we have been persistent during it. May Allah give us the accomplishment of *taqwa* before the end of Ramadan. May Allah accept from us and our family our fasts, *qiyam*, *ruku'*, and *sujud, Allahumma āmīn*. May Allah accept from all of us the blessings that we have sought in order to fulfil our deeds and worship. May Allah سبحانه و تعالى return it to us in the form of a greater *barakah*. May Allah accept our charity through the little that we have offered towards others in our service.

DAY 30

Sunnah of Eid

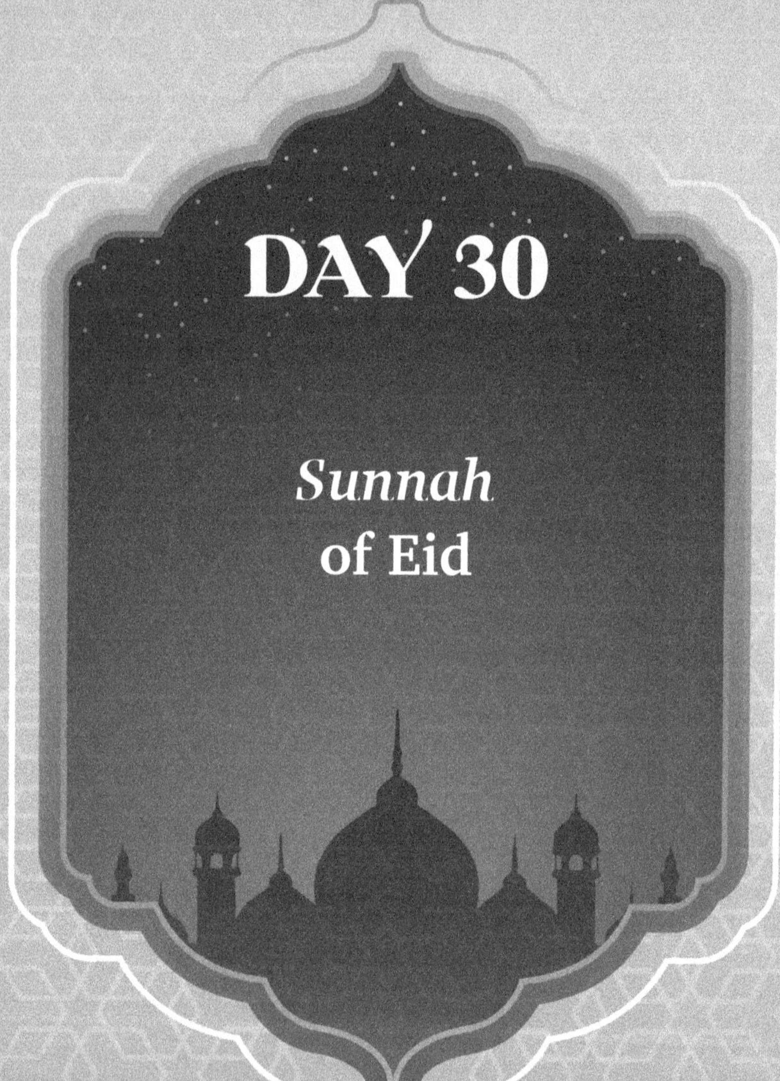

Alhamdulillah, the month of Ramadan has come to an end. We are thankful to encounter the night of Eid, and tomorrow, we shall be able to celebrate our success after a month of training our *iman* and faith. May Allah سبحانه و تعالى give us and our family happiness and joy in it on the day of Eid. We shall observe reminders for some of the *sunnah* of Prophet Muhammad ﷺ on the day of *Eid al-Fitr*.

On the morning of Eid, after we wake up, we should perform *ghusl*, or the ritual bath, for *Eid al-Fitr*. Afterwards, the *sunnah* of Prophet Muhammad ﷺ is to put on nice clothing. The clothing does not necessarily have to be brand new; it should be nicer clothing than you normally wear, or your favourite clothing. Nice clothing is clothing that you believe would be pleasing to Allah, who is the King of kings; it does not have to be new or colourful.

Second, we should ensure that we contribute to create a joyful environment in our homes for our family, wife, and children. One suggestion is to give presents to our loved ones. It could be some extra change that we could gift them; however, the gift does not need to be tangible. It could also be an act of service, or anything we do that could bring a smile to someone's face.

Third, before performing the *Eid al-Fitr* prayer, we

should ensure that we eat some food for breakfast. As we have recently completed fasting for an entire month, one of the first things we should do in the morning, to mark the end of the fasting month, is to eat in the morning after *Fajr*. It is also *sunnah* of Prophet Muhammad ﷺ to eat an odd number of dates; either one, three, five, or seven. We could drink some milk if the house has run out of dates, as we may have run out of dates by the end of Ramadan. Should we have some time to plan, we ought to try our best to have the food that Prophet Muhammad ﷺ consumed on the day of Eid, *inshaa Allah*.

Furthermore, on the day of Eid, men should wear perfumes, or nice-smelling oils. This is the *sunnah* of Prophet Muhammad ﷺ. On the other hand, women should avoid wearing perfumes, or excessively beautifying themselves when they intend to go out of their homes. They are to wear beautiful clothing, similarly to men; however, they should keep their intention to beautify themselves within the compounds of their own home and family.

It should also be noted that whether our wives, daughters, or sisters are able to perform their prayers or not, everyone should highly be encouraged to attend the *Eid al-Fitr* congregational prayers at the *masjid*. It is the *sunnah* of Prophet Muhammad ﷺ to dedicate a part of his *khutbah* especially for women, and invite them to give charity and be kind to one another. This is another *sunnah* to perform on the day of Eid; that we continue to give charity even after the month of Ramadan has ended; not just *zakat al-Fitr*, but giving extra *sadaqah* as much as we can afford to.

Another important sunnah of Eid is to take a different route home than the one we took to head for prayer. Lastly, throughout our day on the day of Eid, whether we are heading to the *masjid* or returning home, we should make *takbir*. The *takbir* that we are encouraged to recite on the day of Eid is:

اَللهُ اَكْبَرُ– اَللهُ اَكْبَرُ– اَللهُ اَكْبَرُ

لآاِلَـهَ اِلاَّاللـهُ وَاللـهُ اَكْبَرُاَللـهُ اَكْبَرُاَللـهُ اَكْبَـرُ

وَلِلـهِ الْحَمْـدُ

Allah is Most Great, Allah is Most Great, Allah is Most Great, there is no god except Allah, Allah is Most Great, Allah is Most Great, Allah is Most Great and all praise be to Allah.

These are some of the great *sunan* of Prophet Muhammad ﷺ to carry out on the day of Eid. May Allah accept our fasts, and our obedience towards Allah. *Barakallahu li wa lakum fi Ramadan. Allahumma taqabbal Ramadan minna*. May Allah سبحانه و تعالى accept all of our deeds throughout Ramadan. *Allahumma ameen.*

This is where I, Yahya Ibrahim, ask the readers to remember me; a weak and sinful brother, in your sincere *du'a*. May Allah grant me, my family, and lineage istiqamah and firmness of heart upon the faith until all of us return to Allah. All that was good in the book are from Allah and the teachings of Prophet Muhammad ﷺ . Any errors are from me and the influence of *shaytan*. Allah سبحانه و تعالى and Prophet Muhammad ﷺ are free from blemishes.

Jazakum Allahu Khair.

Glossary

عليه السلام (**‘alayhi s-salam**): May peace be upon him

Adhan: Announcement; the Muslim call to Friday congregational worship (*Jumu‘ah* prayer) and to the five daily prayers

‘Asr: The time when the shadow of something becomes longer than its shadow at the time of true zenith

Barakah: Blessings; Allah’s blessing or bounty in relation to one’s worldly pursuits. It refers to qualitative growth in one’s possessions.

Da’if: Flawed; despicable; weak

Dhikr: A form of devotion; a mention for remembrance of Allah

Dhuhr: One of the mandatory five daily prayers; the noon prayer; the second prayer of the day

Du‘a: Invocation; an act of supplication

Fajr: The time which the sky starts to become light after night; the first light; daybreak; crack of dawn

Fitrah: The original state in which humans are created by Allah

Hadith: A collection of traditions containing sayings of Prophet Muhammad ﷺ which, with accounts of his daily practice (the *sunnah*), constitute the major source of guidance for Muslims apart from the Qur’an

Halal: Permissible; allowed

Haram: Forbidden

Iman: Faith; belief

Iqamah: The call to prayer made immediately before Muslims pray

Isha': One of the mandatory five daily prayers; the night prayer; the fifth prayer of the day

I'tikaf: A period of staying in a mosque for a certain number of days, devoting oneself to *'ibadah* and staying away from worldly affairs during this time; in Ramadan, it is popularly carried out during the last 10 days

Jahannam: Hellfire

Kalimah: The formal content of the *shahada* (the declaration of faith)

Khutbah: A sermon preached by an *imam* in a mosque, usually at the time of the Friday congregational prayer, Eid, or *nikah*

Lailatul Qadr: The Night of Power; an Islamic occasion that commemorates the night on which Allah first revealed the Qur'an to Prophet Muhammad ﷺ through the angel, Gabriel. It is believed to have taken place on one of the final 10 nights of Ramadan in 610 CE, though the exact night is unclear

Maghrib: One of the mandatory five daily prayers; the prayer that is performed as soon as the sun sets at dusk; the fourth prayer of the day

Masjid: Muslims' place of worship; the house of Allah; house of prayer; place of worship; any building where congregations gather for prayer

رضي الله عنه ***(radhiya -llahu 'anhu/'anha)***: May Allah be pleased with her/him

ﷺ ***(salla -llahu 'alayhi wa-sallam)***: Peace and blessings be upon him (Prophet Muhammad ﷺ)

سبحانه و تعالى ***(subhanahu wa-ta'ala)***: Glory to Allah; glorified and exalted is He

Sadaqah: Charity

Sahabah: The companions; companions of the Prophet Muhammad ﷺ

Shaytan: An unbelieving class of *Jinn*

Suhoor: Pre-dawn meal

Sunnah: The body of traditional, social, and legal custom and practice of the Islamic community; referred to along with the Qur'an and *hadith* (recorded sayings of Prophet Muhammad ﷺ); a major source of *shariah*, or Islamic law.

Surah: Chapters of the Qur'an

Tawaf: The ritual of circumambulating the *Ka'bah* seven times as part of *hajj* or *umrah* in Makkah

Ulama': The body of religious scholars who are versed theoretically and practically in the Muslim sciences

www.ingramcontent.com/pod-product-compliance
Ingram Content Group UK Ltd.
Pitfield, Milton Keynes, MK11 3LW, UK
UKHW021932190726
13853UKWH00004B/1404

9 789672 420996